NO TIME TO BREATHE

Voices from the COVID-19 Pandemic

Kellen Squire RN

FOREWARD

The COVID-19 pandemic reshaped healthcare in unimaginable ways. For those working in hospitals, ambulances, long-term care facilities, and emergency rooms, it was an unrelenting storm that left behind scars—both visible and invisible.

These are the unfiltered, raw, and at times, unbearable experiences of nurses, doctors, paramedics, respiratory therapists, scientists, medical researchers, and other everyday heroes who fought on the frontlines, caring for patients in a time of uncertainty, fear, and overwhelming loss... but even they are just a fraction of what healthcare workers endured.

For many of us, the pandemic didn't just change how we practiced medicine—it changed who we are. Some left healthcare entirely. Some, like me, moved to education, trying to shape a future where healthcare providers don't have to suffer like we did. Others are still fighting, still holding hands, still trying to make a difference.

The post-traumatic stress experienced by frontline healthcare providers during the COVID-19 pandemic has not just been overlooked—it has been actively ignored. In the early days, when hospitals were overwhelmed and providers worked through exhaustion, fear, and grief, there was an outpouring of public support. Politicians called them "healthcare heroes", social media was filled with messages of gratitude, and people clapped from balconies. But as soon as the crisis became inconvenient to acknowledge, as soon as the narrative shifted from emergency to "moving on," those same providers were abandoned to deal with the aftermath alone. The trauma didn't end when the cases declined. The memories of patients dying alone, of impossible choices made without enough resources, of helplessness in the face of an unrelenting virus—those remain. And yet, the moment providers began speaking about what they endured, the world simply stopped listening.

This isn't accidental. Acknowledging the PTSD of COVID providers would mean admitting that we, as a society, allowed them to be sacrificed. It would mean reckoning with the fact that they were forced into war zones without proper protection, that they held iPads for dying patients while families sobbed on the other end, that they absorbed the anger of a public that quickly turned against them when the crisis interfered with their daily lives. Politicians don't want to address it because doing so would mean accepting responsibility for failing them—failing to provide adequate support, failing to protect their mental health, failing to prevent the burnout and mass exodus from healthcare that followed. The public doesn't want to face it because it would mean confronting their own complacency, the way they eagerly applauded from their windows but later refused to wear masks or believed conspiracy theories over the people who fought to save lives.

So instead, the silence continues. PTSD in frontline providers has been medicalized, individualized, treated as if it were the burden of each person to carry alone rather than the result of a systemic failure. No national reckoning, no government-funded mental health support programs, no large-scale recognition of what was endured—just a quiet expectation that they will keep showing up, keep working, keep enduring.

But the trauma remains. And for those who lived it, the hardest thing to accept is not just that the world has moved on, but that it has done so deliberately, leaving them behind with memories too heavy to carry alone.

Across the globe, those who weathered the storm—whether in bustling urban centers or remote communities— need to be able to realize that they are not alone. Sharing these stories is crucial. They weave together a tapestry of resilience and solidarity, reminding us that even in our darkest moments, the bonds of shared struggle and hope endure. By telling these tales, we honor the sacrifices made and offer comfort to those who continue to fight, affirming that our collective experience is both a burden shared and a strength that unites us.

Because none of us came out the same.

Kellen Squire, RN

I remember the exact moment I realized we were all fucked.

It was March. COVID was on the news but it was before lock down.

There was a patient in the ICU with atypical pneumonia. Our critical care doc wanted to check the patient for this new virus.

The state of Florida told us no. The state health department had a limited number of tests, and they would only send one to you if the patient had been outside of the US or on a cruise ship.

And then once lockdown happened and they finally admitted that COVID was a pandemic rapidly spreading, it took a week to get the test results back. We couldn't run them in house. We couldn't run them in state. We had to send them the first several weeks all the way up to Atlanta. And we prioritized testing patients admitted to the ICU. We would admit patients to the hospital for suspicion of COVID but could not test them.

Then remdesivir was announced as a treatment option. We made our ethics committee decide which patient would get the treatment. We usually only got enough supply for maybe 3 patients a day.

I remember the first night the morgue was full.

It was dark times.

I remember watching the news and having the feeling of an oncoming train. Our house growing up was right by the train tracks, Union Pacific would run through there at 55 miles an hour. Before anything else, you could hear this ominous... hear isn't even the right word. It was something deeper, an instinctive stirring in the back of your skull. A resonance that vibrates through your very core. A premonition that rises unbidden, as ominous and inescapable as the rumble itself. It's hard to describe if you haven't experienced it firsthand.

It was here way before it was identified. From the late 2019 into 2020 winter season, we had so many respiratory patients that we just couldn't seem to treat, on ventilators, on high flow oxygen. It wasn't until March when we were thinking it was probably COVID. I live in rural Pennsylvania, so from April till June during the first lockdown, we were really slow and had very few people who were sick. But by the summer it got bad. The first winter was awful. I thought the second winter couldn't be as bad, but 2021 to 2022 was horrific. I ended up leaving ICU for a year and a half because I needed a break from people dying.

I've never forgiven the people who were lucky enough to float through the pandemic, untouched and unconcerned. The people who rolled their eyes at masks, scoffed at overwhelmed hospitals, and carried on with their lives while we drowned in death and despair.

They had the privilege of ignorance. They got to live in bliss while we watched patients choke on their own lungs, while we comforted the dying over FaceTime because their families weren't allowed inside. While we made impossible choices, rationing ventilators and medicine, deciding who might live and who certainly would not.

They got to pretend it wasn't happening. They got to say, "It's just the flu." They got to demand ivermectin while our colleagues buried their parents. They ignored the exhaustion in our eyes when we dared to step outside the hospital walls. And now, years later, they've tried to erase it all— rewriting history to suit their comfort.

But we have not forgotten. The ones who survived carry these stories in their bones, in their nightmares, in the quiet moments when the weight of it all crashes down.

It happened. It all happened. And no amount of willful ignorance can ever change that.

I was working at a very large prison, which was the site of the first outbreak for my state. When we first started getting positive cases, we put them in "medical isolation," which was essentially moving them to one unit in segregation because we didn't know what else to do. I was the charge nurse that day when we got a call about one of the offenders acting weird—usually a sign of drug use—so I had one of the nurses run down there to assess him. She called me back and said that he was mottling- turning purple- and that she couldn't get any vitals on him. I responded, "That sounds like a dead person," but she informed me that he was still talking to her.

At that point, I grabbed another nurse and ran down there with our gurney and emergency kit. Sure enough, he was mottled on his arms and legs, we couldn't get a set of vitals, and she was trying to start an IV- but it wouldn't flush, even though we were definitely in his veins. My doctor said, "Send him out *now*."

This guy was a healthy 30-year-old man with zero previous medical history. He had no symptoms the day before. COVID had caused clots throughout his arms and legs. He ended up going septic, but, from what I heard, he did survive. He eventually returned to our facility about 30 pounds lighter, with permanent damage to his legs and the need for a cane. That was what really made me afraid of COVID.

It eventually spread to half our facility (over 500 people). We had entire units of sick people. Some were completely fine, while others were begging me for help. All I could do was try to comfort them, give them the prescribed medications, and make sure their oxygen was as high as we could manage. The local hospital was refusing to take people from us because they were also full. We were so understaffed already and legally only allowed to work 16 hours, so we'd have to stop what we were doing in the middle of a medication pass and just leave... so some people wouldn't even get their normal medications.

Eventually, the mental health workers were doing rounds just taking temperatures and oxygen levels because there was no way the nurses could assess every sick person in the facility while also taking care of those who were not sick.

But to end the story on a kind note, there was one day when I broke down crying while trying to pass medications because it was so overwhelming- and just to make it worse, one of the patients got mad at me for not having something. Then a week later, a couple of units had raised money to buy all of the medical staff gift certificates to a local restaurant, with handmade cards to go along with them.

Monday, March 20th, 2020:

"Good morning,

As I write this, there are over 5,000 cases of COVID in Michigan, with 132 deaths. And as we know, Detroit has been slammed by this bug and we're hurting.

I'm sipping my coffee right now and I'm filled with anxiety. I'm wondering what this day will bring, and wishing that I could stay home and quarantine like a "non-essential" worker.

But, I'm about to walk into the fire again today. I work (RN) at one of the big hospitals downtown; things are crazy there, and every day it gets worse. More sick, more dying. I cry every day, but every day I dry my tears and vow to get through another day. One day at a time, that's all I can do. That's all any of us can do, really.

I'm not gonna lie - I've thought about quitting, and staying home and staying safe, but I can't do that.

Detroit is in my blood. I was born in the city, my brother was a DPD officer, and dad worked the steel foundries. I've always loved Detroit, even when others didn't, even when outsiders bashed it - I love this city, and the people in it. I always have, and always will. I've taught my sons to love the city, and I've shared many happy memories with them here. Detroit is in their blood too.

Detroiters are a special breed. We have huge hearts and nerves of steel. We are tough, and we are fighters, and we will overcome this challenge like we've overcome so many others. I believe in the spirit of Detroit, the spirit of the people.

I guess I just want you all to know that it's you that I'm getting dressed for today, it's you that I'm drying my tears for and shoving aside my fears for. I love you, Detroit, and I'm going to fight like hell for all of you. We're going to be ok. I believe that.

Stay safe at home. I got this :)"

The thing that struck me about COVID was how many of us became functional alcoholics. It wasn't just my ER, either; I talked to a lot of colleagues across the country and was startled to hear how many times this came up. But I shouldn't have been. If you see that much death, that much suffering, all of it unneeded, unnecessary. I got to where I was glad to go to work, even with the volume we had from COVID, because I knew I couldn't be drunk on the clock. So I'd have a breather where I had a fixed reason why I couldn't drink, couldn't talk myself into it, etc.

I look back on it now, and I was drinking a startling amount. Like a lot. A lot a lot. I'm afraid to even write down here how much. And how many other nurses were in the same exact boat. But I don't know how else I would have made it through myself.

I worked in the ER in Oakland county, Michigan. On one shift, I watched 11 patients die. No family at their side, no final words… just gasping for breath, no ventilators available. For protection, we were wrapped in garbage bags that my coworkers taped to my body. We ran out of PPE, we were buying our own supplies. The next day I saw 10 patients die in the ER. The paramedics and EMTs that brought these patients in waited in the hallways and held the hands of those dying on their stretchers because we didn't have a bed to put the patients in. I have PTSD and will NEVER work in a hospital again.

I worked in long term care during COVID, so my experience was a bit different but still traumatic. When the shutdown happened, families weren't allowed to see their loved ones. Dementia residents became increasingly depressed; many stopped eating. Then COVID swept through the building—each unit of 20 lost 8–10 residents. Families had to say goodbye from outside the window or over an iPad. The skilled residents came to us more acutely because hospitals needed to open beds. One morning, we had 3 codes within an hour, which was unheard of in SNF/LTC before COVID.

Then the staffing shortage hit, and nursing leadership was working 24-hour shifts because there was no one else to fill in. I worked multiple shifts with just myself and one CNA for 20 residents. Some shifts had only 1–2 CNAs and 2 nurses for 64 residents. We even had a beloved CNA take his own life after clocking out from his night shift. I came out of it all with clinical depression. I wanted to leave nursing and never look back. I still feel like it's nothing compared to what the nurses at hospitals were dealing with.

(I weathered COVID in the ICU and I want you to know that doesn't sound like nothing to me. You are incredibly strong for getting through that, and I'm sorry it was asked of you.)

I was an ER nurse floated to assist in ICU at a rural hospital, where the typical ICU patient was over 80 years old. The patient I had, though, was a male in his 50s; the primary nurse was 24/25 yrs old max. Patient was vented and dying. We went to prone them, to flip them on their belly, and the patient went into SVT. The primary nurse called the wife who was home with COVID and asked if we could get a priest to give last rights.

We couldn't find a damn priest to come in. We called the on-call priest and every parish in the area, including his own priest. No one came.

He died. Without any family, hand held by a nurse who was lost in all of it, had never had a patient this young die.

That's when I knew we were alone, healthcare workers were alone, no one was coming to help, no one was coming to save us.

I got COVID three weeks after I started a job at a facility in 2020. The facility had been running out of gloves, didn't have gowns, and we weren't properly fitted for N95 masks. This was a time where we had been doing weekly testing of all staff and patients. I remember thinking "next wave I'm going to get it" and then 3 patients I had been assigned to tested positive. I tested positive the following week. I spent the rest of the week prior to my positive test watching rooms empty and walking through silent hallways. I started feeling symptoms and had to self-report until my positive results came back.

When I came back to work 2 weeks later, my entire wing was empty. All of the patients had tested positive during one of the waves and were sent out.

Delta was as bad as everyone says, sometimes worse. Things I won't forget about delta are the COVID units, or half a floor being commandeered as COVID rooms. We didn't have the room for them anywhere else. The body bags, BAGS plural. We had monitors set up, we watched families grieve.

The miscarriages. You never heard those on the news, but the miscarriages. We had more miscarriages in 2020 than I've seen for the rest of my career combined. Both Labor and Delivery and the NICU have these teeny tiny little boxes for when they have a death. We ran out. We ran out of all of them. I remember working one day, and one of our techs began screaming on the radio from the triage bathroom. A mom had been waiting for three hours- we had probably ten hour waits that day, easy- and miscarried right there in the waiting room bathroom. It looked like a fucking horror movie. Clots everywhere. Screaming.

I got COVID three weeks after I started a job at a facility in 2020. The facility had been running out of gloves, didn't have gowns, and we weren't properly fitted for N95 masks. This was a time where we had been doing weekly testing of all staff and patients. I remember thinking "next wave I'm going to get it" and then 3 patients I had been assigned to tested positive. I tested positive the following week. I spent the rest of the week prior to my positive test watching rooms empty and walking through silent hallways. I started feeling symptoms and had to self-report until my positive results came back.

When I came back to work 2 weeks later, my entire wing was empty. All of the patients had tested positive during one of the waves and were sent out.

The Delta strain was as bad as everyone says, sometimes worse. Things I won't forget about Delta are the COVID units, or half a floor being commandeered as COVID rooms. We didn't have the room for them anywhere else. The body bags, BAGS plural. We had monitors set up, we watched families grieve.

Worked in the ER in a busy urban area in the northeast. We got hit early and hard. I honestly don't like talking about it. I ended up the only nurse in the ER hospitalized (for 8 days). It wasn't fun.

I worked in long-term care during COVID. We lost half of our residents, many of whom I'd cared for for years. My husband worked there too. At night, we each had a whole unit and split another. We'd start rounding from opposite ends and work toward the middle. There was only time to hit each room once. People would grab my sleeve, begging me to kill them or just let them die.

Then we'd go home to our daughters—one just a few months old—and pray we didn't bring it home to them or my mom, who has a long history of lung problems. I lost my dad to COVID later that year. I live in a red area, and half the people I worked with are antivaxxers, even after everything we saw. At least one told me my dad's death proved "the vaccines don't work," never mind his long-term health issues.

I became a hardcore alcoholic for a while—two years sober and counting. I worked for a small nonprofit hospice to heal from COVID's impact. I needed time to hold hands, talk to families, and do the things I couldn't when people were dying left and right. It helped me a lot and reminded me why I liked healthcare.

Neither my husband nor I work in healthcare right now. I plan to go back eventually; he's undecided. We were passionate about it, but it's a hard job for people as sensitive as we are. And at our level of education, it just doesn't pay enough to endure what we did.

I was doing acute inpatient dialysis. Got called in after I'd already worked a full shift day to run a treatment on an emergency new-start patient with multiple organ failure. from COVID. 45 year old father of two. I rolled into the ICU to find a bank of IV pumps set up- sedatives, every blood pressure med known to man, heparin to thin his blood, maybe even remdesevir (but I don't remember if it was out yet). Hail Mary dialysis.

This man clotted my dialysis machine in less than 10 minutes *on a heparin drip*. I couldn't even believe it. Set up again and almost immediately saw signs of clotting. Started tweaking machine settings and flushing the system w/saline every ten minutes or so, trying everything I could think of to get this treatment completed without losing the blood again. (Clotted system = lost one unit of blood. Couldn't afford to let him lose a second unit.)

I managed to drag him through an hour and a half before I had to stop because I was afraid I wouldn't be able to rinse his blood back. He died the next morning. I can't forget that room.

My team had some success with patients who had kidney failure already *prior* to getting COVID. But if they had new kidney failure caused by COVID, we lost all of them. We did not save one single patient in that condition the entire first months of the pandemic before the vaccine was released.

Lovely gentleman walking around the room at the start of my shift, talking to his family on the phone.

He did everything I asked as his O2 requirements increased throughout the night; he even let us flip him prone without complaint.

There was nowhere to send him; all critical care units were overfilled and understaffed. Such a lovely man.

He died the next day.

92-year-old beautiful lady, isolated from her family. She told me, "I know I'm old and going to die but I don't want to die from THIS."

She did anyway.

Interestingly, I don't remember much of the deniers. My brain couldn't even process their stupidity and my heart was already overfull.

It's 5am. I'm waiting.

EMS rolls in with a 72 year old. Shortness of breath.

I have suction ready to go.

"Hey Mike?"

His eyes flutter open.

"We're going to put a tube down your throat and breathe for you, okay?"

Mike breathes at 50 times a minute. The sweat drips off forehead on to the non rebreather.

I mentally swing through the things I have available. It's not much.

I have an airway bag. Two tubes, two blades, one stylette, and a scalpel. We can't bag, because we're out of viral filters, and my attending is outside of the room because we don't have enough masks.

The pulse ox screams at me. 65%.

Don't miss.

While we're drawing meds, Mike stops breathing. Respiratory arrest.

I put his bed down and jaw thrust. He winces and gives me a few breaths.

I'm not a panicky person.

The panic bubbles.

"We need to push meds. Let's go."

The one nurse, one tech, and one RT we have in the room look at me. I know they know this.

I breathe in through the layer of an N95, surgical mask, face shield.

Slow is smooth. Smooth is fast. I'm not a panicky person.

I stop thinking about how my back up plan is immediately for a scalpel. Meds are pushed and I shove suction in and take a look.

It takes me exactly 8 seconds to the time he's getting his first intubated breath. His pulse ox reads 45%.

I breathe through the layers. Slow is smooth. I watch his spo2 creep up to the 80s and I sigh.

"I'm sorry, Les. I didn't mean to snap."

His nurse looks near tears. She has three very sick COVID patients under her care now. I think maybe there's a contract nurse somewhere to help her, but she's busy.

I step out of the room and put in orders. His CXR looks like everyone else's.

I grab the ultrasound machine and make my way to the room of a 32 year old COVID positive patient who's here for vaginal spotting. Jenny.

Before EMS frantically gave us the heads up about the Shortness. Of. Breath. I had spent a few minutes talking with Jenny.

She was twenty weeks pregnant wirh her second baby. A week of a cough and chills brought her to her OB's office two days ago, where she was swabbed and found to be COVID positive. She tried to stay away from everyone, but a few drops of blood anxiously brought her to the ED.

I gown up. Same N95, different surgical mask. Same eye shield, different gown. I push the ultrasound through and make sure there are wipes in stock today so that I can actually clean it after.

"Hey again, Jenny! Let's take a peek at the baby!"

It's never just not there.

I always find fetal heart tones.

Twenty weeks?

There's always fetal heart tones.

I stare far too long at the motionless heart. I mentally swing through my options. I can't get a formal ultrasound on a COVID positive patient. Will OB even seen her in the department? The panic bubbles.

"Jenny, do you have anyone here with you?"

"My husband is outside. They told him he couldn't come in." She twists her wedding ring.

"Jenny, I have bad news. Do you want me to call your husband so he can hear too?"

She starts sobbing.

I tell her that I couldn't find a heartbeat. OB will recheck, but your baby, Jenny, has died.

I am so sorry.

She shouldn't be alone for this. I ask charge to let her husband back, and they refuse. Hospital policy.

I sit with Jenny for as long as I can. I hold her hand through two layers of gloves. His name was going to be Mike. The name isn't lost on me. I sit there for about three minutes.

The EMS radio blares. Shortness. Of. Breath. Will need tube.

I squeeze Jenny's hand and give her the in room phone. I am so sorry.

I pull everything off except the N95. That stays for five shifts.

I walk in to the next room and grab suction.

I'm not a panicky person.

I was a paramedic and firefighter throughout the pandemic in a very sick and violent city. I remember the first night it "really broke out." We had to wear full Tyvex suits and N95 masks. My city is already lacking in hospitals on a good day, but my very first call for COVID had me waiting in a line of ambulances outside an ER for 8 hours. Just me and a sick patient sitting in the parking lot for what felt like an eternity.

Once we got inside, every room had patients on some sort of oxygen delivery device. Some were on ventilators; others non-rebreathers. Patients lined the hallways taking up every inch of wall real estate. Us medics and EMTs started trying to help where we could. Getting lines on patients brought in without one and doing triage work all while still being in eyeshot of our patient that we were still responsible for. It took another 2 hours to be able to offload my patient, finish my documentation, and get right back out there for another one.

I don't know how long things continued this way. It's all a blur now. At some point we were told we didn't need the Tyvex suits anymore, but we were no longer supposed to intubate or aerosol anyone in the field. Of course we all still did.

There were a lot of very sick people. Some imminently dying, others just feeling like they were. For the most part I think people were scared. It wasn't uncommon to get a 911 call simply for "I tested positive," and their vitals and disposition both good - but they were scared and didn't know what to do. I gave out a lot of IV fluids and Ondansetron anti-nausea medication in attempts to keep people out of the hospitals that really didn't need to go.

I picked up quite a few younger people that had serious problems either following COVID or the vaccine. I don't know what the answer is, and I'm not here to talk politics.

One was a 28 year old crossfitter that told me "I can't see." He had literally lost his eyesight. CT scans showed a stroke upon arrival, although no other symptoms at the time led me towards a CVA.

Had a 36 year old father of 3 drop dead in his garage. I was not able to get ROSC on him, but damn we tried. I responded a week later to the same house for his wife having a panic attack and she cried when she saw me saying "I know you were the one who came for him." Broke my heart.

I have a lot of others, but truthfully I know I am forgetting just as many if not more. I was completely burnt out by late 2021 and have not worked in emergency medicine since.

Our pulmonologist lost it on a family member who said, "Why don't you try ivermectin?! You haven't even tried it!" He responded, "Well, why don't I try just taking a huge shit on them too?! I haven't tried that either, but I know it won't work!"

Part of me felt bad for the family, but I definitely get where our pulmonologist was coming from. The poor guy was working every single day, trying his best to come up with SOMETHING to get patients off the vent. We were all overworked and being treated like shit.

I worked in the first hospital in Utah that got their first COVID patient on my floor as a CNA. We were all terrified.

A month later we became the COVID backup floor. I wore a PAPR hood my entire shift, I never got breaks because we didn't have time. I saw people die from complications often. I had to sit with confused patients doing 1:1s in a PAPR because there was no other choice.

I got the Delta variant in 2021, before I was working for a hospital and I was teaching PreK. My aide showed up with what she claimed was a cold, but turned out to be COVID and she'd refused to mask up. I had gotten both vaccine doses and thought I was fine and had my flu shot.

However, within two days I ended up in the hospital; I had been helping out in another classroom and passed out. Our director refused to call me an ambulance, so after coming to I drove myself to the hospital. I was struggling to breathe and my heart was doing double time, I ended up with a BP of 172/110, a fever of 102.4. I was admitted to the COVID ward for 5 days. I thought at one point that I'd die there and had ripped out my IV and monitor because I didn't want to die there. They were stretched so thin the CNAs barely had time to help change linen or get anything for patients.

I watched two people die next to me, one was a 38 year old nutritionist and gym owner; the other a 52 year old veteran. Both were healthy and fit people. I'll never forget any of the staff, working so hard to save them and then learning that they had died despite everything. It was so utterly heartbreaking and surreal, I remember when I got cleared to go home and the cardiologist doing a final ultrasound, telling me that I'm a miracle and to thank any Gods there may be as I made it when so many others didn't.

I had a lot stacked against me with chronic illnesses, being chubby, and asthmatic. These stories need to be told. I don't know if the two next to me were vaccinated. All I knew was the little I had been told or what I had heard. No one deserved to die like that over a vaccine that could make a difference. Get vaccinated!

I had been a nurse for a few years and moved from MedSurg to the Medical ICU summer of 2019. During the pandemic we became the COVID ICU. There are so many crazy stories from that time. Lots of incredibly sad events like holding people's hands as they passed away because families weren't allowed to visit. Families saying their goodbyes over FaceTime with the iPads we got for the units. Reusing N95s for a week and keeping them in a brown bag on the unit.

Multiple times, patients in our ICU had their husband/wife in the ICU at the other hospital nearby. Their condition would stabilize, but then we'd have to watch the look on their faces after the team told them their loved one didn't make it.

Getting called all sorts of names and getting threats by COVID deniers— either over the phone or by patients themselves. Then watching those same deniers beg for the vaccine as their oxygen saturations were in the 50s and we were getting ready to intubate them.

Putting patients on a maxed-out high flow nasal cannula and then also putting a 100% non-rebreather mask over it to push as much oxygen in them and keep them from being intubated. And that actually worked- sometimes.

Had a lady who was only stable on her ventilator while in a Trendelenburg position (feet was up, head way down). The moment you laid her flat, the vent would go nuts, screaming warnings. We couldn't feed her since she was upside down. Her family made her "comfort measures only" and she passed away.

A guy whose body was rotting from the inside out- literally pooping out the lining of his intestines. Just looked and smelled like a corpse but was fully awake. Somehow stabilized and was transferred to the floor but coded and died a couple days later.

There's lots more that I can't even remember... or probably repressed in some way to cope with what happened during that time.

I do not consider myself a COVID vet. I was working in the hospital during COVID, but as a NICU nurse we generally considered ourselves "lucky" that we were fairly insulated from the other areas of the hospital that we knew got hit a lot harder.

The smallest baby I ever cared for was a 310 gram 28-weeker. Mom had a COVID infection around 19–20 weeks and severe intrauterine growth restriction developed after that. Per the delivery team, the placenta was full of clots. Baby lived maybe a week and a half.

Last year we did an emergency c-section on a mom who came in for reduced fetal movement, who was in her late second trimester. Had COVID a couple weeks earlier, but otherwise had an uneventful pregnancy. It was under general anesthesia so dad had to wait outside. Baby came out and... I don't want to be too explicit here, but it was very obvious he was not going to live. The bedside blood values, the baby's hemoglobin and hematocrit, were unreadable. We brought dad in, and anesthesia had to bring mom out of it quickly so that she could hold their baby while he passed.

It's forever burned into my mind how the mom woke up and frantically asked, "Is the baby okay?"

Our neonatologist essentially said it was coagulopathy secondary to COVID infection, but we'll never really know. When babies are born that early the coroner rarely thinks an autopsy is necessary, and most parents understandably decline one.

That's the hardest part for me. I know that I can't say definitively anything I saw was the result of COVID. There just isn't enough research and solid data, and now there certainly won't be any moving forward. But ANYONE working maternity/NICU during COVID can attest that we saw a lot of weird shit.

And this is on top of the secondary effects of hospitals being absolutely ravaged by COVID. Like having to care for a little guy whose mom died after nobody showed up to the rapid response, because they were all too busy with other patients in similar dire straits.

Anyway, now I get to hear from random people how there is a class action lawsuit against the manufacturers of the COVID vaccine because "all these harmful effects are starting to come out."

I used the same masks for weeks. We used trash bags for gowns. I once lost 16 patient in a day (getting yelled at in between by people asking for ice or blankets). I lied and told people they would be fine, I chased naked people down the hall, I played recordings of prayers for patients on my phone, I prayed to gods I don't worship, I had a chair thrown at me because "the ventilator was killing the patient." I worked 16 hour days, I spent Christmas with COVID. I try not to think about it. I try to pretend it was just a fever dream. It was a defining moment and if it happens again, I quit.

I remember the first patient we got, before things began to shut down, Dry cough, no smell, couldn't taste. This was before we instantly recognized those as symptoms, before we thought it could truly be here. I was in triage. Patient walked in and sat down at my triage desk, and I put the oxygen probe on their finger. Their oxygen was at 50%. I didn't believe it. I couldn't believe it because they were just sitting there typing on their cell phone. What we didn't know then was that COVID screwed with people a couple ways. You blew off your carbon dioxide like normal, so your body doesn't respond to make you feel really short of breath. There's some other things involving V/Q mismatch and chemoreceptors but long story short, these patients were literally dying right in front of us and they had no idea. We called it "happy hypoxia". Anyway I checked this patient's oxygen on three machines in triage before it clicked. I can't even describe the cold dread and almost panic. I think that's why they found so many people dead at home. They had no idea until it was too late. Right at the end it seemed like the body figured out what was going on. Which means these people panicked when it finally hit them. The terror, I can't even think about what they went through.

One of the main hospitals in our county completely stopped accepting patients, even from ambulances, no matter the severity, for multiple consecutive days at a time. If EMS had a pediatric cardiac arrest, they would not accept it. They would have to be transported to the next closest hospital 20 miles away.

They did this twice. Once for 6 straight days, once for 9 days, I believe, in 2020/2021. They didn't just run out of rooms. They ran out of beds. And chairs. This is "COVID denier" country too. I live amongst a bunch of raving idiots.

One of our charge nurses was a raving antivaxxer. You couldn't get within ten feet of her without hearing a screed about it. She managed to stick around through the COVID vaccine mandate by claiming religious reasons and promising to wear an N95 without fail during every shift. Total shock: she didn't do that, and ended up getting COVID.

She actually handled getting COVID okay, but she gave it to her mom. And her mom did not handle it at all. About a week in, she came into our ER, and got admitted to the COVID unit. And then decompensated, and headed to the ICU. One night, I'm on call, and at about 2AM I get a panicked call from the unit secretary that I need to come into the ER now, that the charge nurse had run out of the department screaming, and demanded one of the ER doctors come with her.

Turns out what had happened was that they'd called a Code Blue on her mom, who was going into respiratory arrest. I'm not sure what she thought our ER doc was going to add to the mix. And they left a full ER with only a single nurse practitioner on duty and no charge nurse, which I can only imagine is illegal as hell, not to mention dangerous.

I get it was her mom. I can only imagine. But, still.

Her mom died in the ICU that night. But how do you tell someone who is so clearly devastated that they were the reason their mom died, and that they endangered the lives of dozens of other patients in doing so?

There's no joy in "toldjasos" though.

The last COVID story I am just now beginning to tell. And yes I know I should have quit way before I did.

A five year old child was set to go to Kindergarten. Her grandparents, who were from somewhere in Central America, were concerned the child was going to get sick. So they gave the child AN ENTIRE TUBE OF IVERMECTIN HORSE DEWORMER.

The child died. By the time the child became sick at school it was too late to do anything.

This after case upon case upon case of people drinking or inhaling bleach, taking horse dewormer, getting in the faces of our critical care staff and threatening them over their refusal to administer bleach, quinine, or ivermectin. Those things I might have been able to handle.

I never went back to work again. I'd been planning on retiring by the end of the year anyway.

I have zero doubt we will see stuff like this again.

A lot of things happened during COVID, but the one that still haunts me when I sleep is this:

We had a patient that was dying from COVID, and finally, the time came for a compassionate extubation. Take the patient off the breathing machine and let them pass as peacefully as possible, without a tube down their throat. The instructions I was given at the time to let someone compassionately die was to remove the tube WITH A BAG OVER HER HEAD to protect myself.

Let me tell you, I loaded this person up with drugs so there would be zero chance they'd have any awareness of that. They were on drugs, but I gave them absolutely everything I was allowed to.

That picture will never leave me. The feeling of having to do that will haunt me forever.

Fuck.

At the start of the pandemic I worked prehospital Fire/EMS as a paramedic. I had just graduated medic school in February and I was a 19 year old medic, so I was considerably young.

October of 2020 I had quit and started working at a Level 2 Trauma center in the ED, as a medic, that is local to where I am from. I remember being on the floor the first day and being told I wasn't allowed to have an N95 mask due to the shortage. I, however, stole it and used that mask for literally 3 weeks.

The amount of patients I saw die from November of 2020 to April of 2022 is staggering. I do not remember them all. However, there are a few that stand out and stick with me. The constant sound of vents, CPAP from EMS, IV pumps is literally stuck in my head to this day.

I walked into the morgue at the peak of the delta wave. We normally had 6 carts to place the body on in the freezer until the bodies were shipped off somewhere. This time, I remember bodies being stacked like jenga blocks. The entire timeline of it feels like a dream, honestly. Actually today, I looked at my schedule from that time because I genuinely couldn't remember if I worked there that much or if I am making it up. I am not. I worked 4-5 12 hour shifts a week because I was taking advantage of the "COVID pay" they offered at the time. There were multiple days that I saw and ran codes in the double digits while only surviving off of tiny peanut butter cups and graham crackers. I'm sure there is so many other stories I can tell you they just don't want to come out for whatever reason.

The reason I found this is because I was out to dinner with a friend and smelt bleach and alcohol mixed together and for whatever reason it made me so uncomfortable I cut them off mid-sentence and told them we had to leave. I don't remember my drive home after that. I am shifting through experiences posted on here because I literally feel insane right now. There is no studies about the trauma HCWs went through during COVID and it is very concerning to me that there is such a substantial amount of a lack of data. I know this is an old post but it feels nice to see the experience validated in this way.

I'm a CT Technologist. Seeing the ravaged lungs of COVID patients with my own eyes every shift, and then hearing people say COVID was fake was certainly wild. I wanted to take them to work with me and then ask them if they still thought it was fake.

I worked in the ICU and cardiac unit. We got floated to the COVID ICU every other shift. Saw a lady lose her husband and dad in the same week. Two new moms never got to hold their babies and died. One said goodbye through a glass door. Watched people give up on living that couldn't breathe while on high flow cannulas with a non-rebreather on top. We were rationing ventilators and medicines, our doctors were so demoralized having to decide who got life saving treatments and who didn't. It was the end of my hospital nursing career. I'm in nursing education now. I will not go back to bedside. We do most of our clinical rotations in the nursing homes. If Medicaid is drastically cut I worry for the long term facilities. The students mostly study with loans and financial aid which is under fire as well. Not sure what I will be doing next year.

We were using so much oxygen that the oxygen lines to the hospital froze.

I am a hospital social worker.

I was pregnant and in my third trimester in March 2020 when COVID hit my area. I was told by hospital admin not to wear a mask because "it would trap the virus and make it more likely for me to get it." I did get COVID and was sent home, getting daily check-ins by employee health and my OBGYN's office by phone. One day the OB called me and listened to my breathing over the phone. They said they didn't like my respiratory rate and told me to go immediately to the ER. It was 6 hours from the time I walked into the ER to me having an emergency c-section at 32 weeks and 6 days pregnant. I was told by my care team that if I had waited 1 more day to come to the ER they would have been doing an emergency c-section at the bedside while I was intubated in the ICU. My son was in the NICU for 3 weeks and I was not allowed to visit him because I was still testing positive until the day he was able to discharge home. I was not allowed to see or hold my son until he was 3 weeks old.

Our Infectious Disease team was able to get me convalescent Remdesivir, which I responded well to, and I was able to discharge home 3 days after the birth. Unfortunately that infectious disease doctor contracted COVID himself and recently passed away from long term complications of the disease.

I remember flipping over a guy who had been in a prone position so long he had a pressure injury to his septum. You could see all of his nasal bones.

I saw 200 people die between April 2020-May 2021.

I was the only person in the room for most of their deaths.

Right at the start of our first big surge, our entire cardiac catheterization lab went down with COVID. The most experienced doc got it so bad, he ended up in our ICU. He came in and was crying, bawling, sure he was going to die. He almost did. We had one, just a single doctor, who could run the entire cath lab during that time. If we had two patients who came in simultaneously having a heart attack, I mean... tough luck, I guess?

The real kicker came six weeks later when the same goddamn thing happened at the hospital across town. Their entire cath lab, save one person, went down. It was only by the grace of God that both of us didn't get hit at the very same time. It could have been worse, the hospital across the mountain from us had to turn their cardiac cath lab into a COVID ICU and ship anyone having a heart attack our direction, a minimum of 30-40 minutes away.

I wrote this sometime in the middle of the pandemic while working on a COVID floor. It's more a poem of general feelings that developed rather than an anecdote, but it's the truth all the same.

"The first time a patient died on me, it hit me hard. That little sweet comfort care grandma was suffering, and it was better this way, but a part of me grieved with her. That was a random Wednesday in March of 2018.

The second time it happened, a patient who had been through the wringer had stopped breathing in the middle of the night. We did compressions on her frail frame, ribs cracking through the skin to no avail. This one hurt more, but when my charge asked me how I felt, I told her the truth. "It's just Wednesday."

The third time was another comfort; she passed alone in the middle of the night. I wanted to weep, but it was just Wednesday.

Then COVID hit: at first I watched so many struggle but not pass, tortured by their own mortal coil. Some would be transferred to another bed. Some got transferred in a body bag. It's just another Wednesday, I tell myself.

But soon Tuesday is Wednesday, and Friday is Wednesday, and Sunday is Wednesday, and Wednesday is Wednesday, and how is it that I've been here for six days straight and it's still Fucking Wednesday!

I am numb to it; I am blind. I remembered their name once upon a godless time. I scream for it, but my voice is hoarse and faded.

Murderer! They call me, giving poison of Decadron and Remdesivir. Satan! They scream, proning their mother instead of just giving her vitamin D. They threaten my life for the simple act of caring for their loved ones. It's just Wednesday.

It's the end of a shift; everyone is safe and sound. I'm calm, thankful for a break. I hand them off to come back tomorrow, and despite leaving on Saturday I round in the morning to find out it's another Wednesday.

The names escape me, as do the numbers. People are screaming: "It's a Wednesday in 62! It's Wednesday in 49! It's Wednesday in 80!"

I start to wonder how a year can have 365 days, and 300 of them be Wednesday.

I need a break; a vacation eases the bruise but leaves the festering sore untouched.

My manager has noticed; I'm truant, distant, I snap easier than I did. Mandatory therapy or a pink slip, my choice.

I choose the therapy. They're nice, warm, kind even. They tell me I'm safe, they tell me they understand: but how can they understand the screams that keep me up at night! Without living this, how can you understand how many graveyards have been filled? How can you understand that I don't dream anymore because any hope I had died a long time ago.

I sigh. I take a deep breathe and speak.

"It's just another Wednesday.""

I worked as an epidemiologist from the first case in Utah to the end of Omicron. I saw everything, from the first Diamond Princess passengers quarantine to breakthrough cases after the vaccine rollout for Pfizer and Moderna. I have thousands of stories, but I'll leave you with the most gutting. I had a case of two grandparents who contracted COVID from one of their grandkids involved in an outbreak on a cheerleading team. Grandma fell severely ill, intubated,ventilated, ecmo, and medically induced coma. I spoke to her husband, and through the tears and fear, he asked if he'd be okay because he was terrified of suffering his wife's fate. I did my best to reassure him; I did my best to give him statistical and epidemiological data i had collected to make him feel prepared for whatever was to come. He became gravely I'll, intubated, ventilated, and finally succumbed to ARDS. I followed up with the family and was updated on his passing. His wife, however, did not die. She finally recovered and had suffered amnesia from the coma she was in for months. she suffered long-term complications from her illness that required her to use an oxygen tank. Out of all her suffering, the most haunting reality is that the person she loved her entire life was alive before she closed her eyes and gone when she awoke. I was angry that the family minimized their contributions to the grandparents fate. I was angry that these two lovely people were so thankful their grandkids recovered, not realizing the imminent danger they were in. What's worse is that their story is not unique. Many people lost their lives. These people died alone, sometimes only comforted by hospital staff. If you haven't done so yet, please thank a HCW because they are the true heart and soul that fought this pandemic.

I personally suffer from PTSD from the pain so many people have faced during COVID. Families losing their homes after being hospitalized for months. Children losing parents. Grandparents dying alone In their homes. It wrecked me. At the end of Omicron, all I was doing was tallying the dead. Without enforcement of public health measures, all we were doing was counting bodies..I felt that my position was pointless...anyone can count the dead. So I left. I lost 20% of the hair on my head to alopecia, which I developed during the pandemic. When I had the chance to leave, I took it. Never looked back. No administration can erase the work our PHW and HCW did during the pandemic. 1 million Americans were erased. ~245k children orphaned. As much as Trump and his cronies would love to wish COVID away, they simply can't. It's been hard to revisit the anguish, but articulating our response is necessary. I was not a HCW, NO ONE saw the work you did. But PH was your brother in arms, I assure you. Thank you to every single HCW. Please know that we are so lucky to have you in our society. You are the backbone of this country. You heal us when we are sick, and you do so blindly, knowing your life too is at risk. Thank you from the bottom of my heart. Your pain and struggle is not lost on me.

Did my initial critical care field training during the first summer after lockdown. When it really hit us, I was working 80 hour weeks, transporting proned, vented patients to wait for ECMO beds DAILY. Some were old and had plenty of comorbidities, but many were my age. And unvaccinated, coming from critical access hospitals where people barely wore masks and flaunted their vax exemptions as an expression of liberty even while they treated people dying in front of them.

I took three incredibly complex pre-ecmo patients (think 3-8 drips, paralyzed, vented, ARDS PEEP levels, balloon pumps, blood, etc) on three consecutive days to the same room on the same unit. The first day I was optimistic. The second day I thought maybe an ECMO bed had opened up for them. The third day I realized that in the time between me dropping them off, clocking out and going home, and coming back to work, all three had died.

On the 911 side, I responded to several patients who would fight with me as much as their hypoxia would allow to bring their ivermectin, to scream at me (where they got the energy for that, I don't know) about how liberals were ruining the country, and who would rip off their bipap mask to harangue me about vaccination status. There were plenty of non-assholes, just sweet, scared older folks, people just wanting a checkup and some reassurance. But it was the awful ones who stood out.

I don't have any regrets about trying to save anyone's life, but in retrospect, I do wish I'd spent less of my precious energy going out of my way to be kind to them in the face of their vitriol. I know that most of them were scared and that's why they were being so awful, but I was scared too.

At the very beginning of the pandemic, I was working in community health. I had clients I would see daily or every few days for years on end. Making up names here for privacy reasons; but I go visit Sally at the retirement home for her foot wound. As I walk in the door, I see stressed looking staff. Two seniors are sick with a cough. They suspect it's COVID but doctors aren't testing people who haven't travelled, so, they don't know. They had a visitor last week who had travelled.

I go see Sally. I'm doing her toe wound and she says to me, "I'm afraid of this virus. I don't think I'll live if I get it, and I'm not ready to die". After work I head to the states to pick up a package a friend sent to my uncle's house there.

The next day I'm working, and I get an email from my boss that anyone who has travelled out of the country has to isolate for two weeks. I call my boss and she says I have to isolate. I lock myself in my basement for two weeks and watch the news.

I get out on a Sunday. I go for a hike. Monday I go to work and back to that retirement home. Every second or third door has droplet precautions signs. I go see Janet. Janet loves to play games in the game room. She's very social. She has a boyfriend Tony who lives in the home as well. I know all the people who play bingo and do the activities because frequently she is doing one when I show up and I sit and wait for her to finish before doing her dressing. I've handed out colouring books and pencil crayons to them. I chat with them. I like these people.

I go up with Janet to her room and she says to me "Sheri, I'm afraid of this virus. I won't live if I get it and I don't want to die". And I'm fucking terrified. I'm immunocompromised. I'm positive this building has COVID. I'm wearing a mask but it doesn't feel like enough. I get out of there so quickly I even forget to chart. I don't go back in to chart. I call my boss from the parking lot. "We need PPE for visits at this place. They've got COVID. I'm sure of it. She says "you're fine. Wear a mask." I tell her I think she's going to kill me and I ask to be laid off. She puts me on a leave of absence. The next day she calls me and says "Sheri. That place is in COVID outbreak. You have to isolate". I lock myself back into my basement room. I turn the news on again. By the third week of isolation, I hear about the facility being in outbreak for COVID. I hear a lot of them have died. They're being criticized for doing what every other retirement home is doing. I open the obituaries and see 19 people I know on the front page. My two clients. Tony. Lots of other residents that I have chatted with over the past decade of being in this building every day I work.

I broke. I could not leave my house for months after this. I couldn't go to the grocery store without having an emotional breakdown. I couldn't handle people being near me. I finally go back to work when things calm down a bit and they seem to have enough PPE.

Community health nurses don't qualify for COVID shots as they aren't tied to a facility so we only get them after "caretakers" and visiting family members do. I've got one shot and I feel semi OK with being back at work. I learn I'm eligible for a booster and I catch COVID from a client who is asymptomatic before I can get it. I spent a month testing positive. I am in bed for two months. I am off work or on reduced hours for six months.

I am a level of tired I have never been in my life for six months. I consider suicide. Life like this is not worth living.

7 months later my energy clicks back on mid day. On a Wednesday. My blood pressure has been high ever since. I am diabetic now.

My energy level sucks. I feel shitty and tired all the time. I've had colds worse than the pneumonia I had when I was younger several times now.

I know this isn't shit compared to what hospital nurses went through. But I liked these people. I knew them. I genuinely cared about them before they got COVID.

After the vaccines came out I would go to the retirement homes in COVID outbreak. I'd ask how they were holding up and how many were in hospital. "Only the unvaccinated go to hospital now"

And then I have to deal with my kid telling me that the COVID vaccination is bullshit and COVID is a lie. And I wanna choke the living shit out of him.

We routinely ran out of body bags so we wrapped the dead up in industrial-sized black trash bags

You ever hear a blood curdling scream over an iPad when you take someone's husband of 40+ years off life support but we couldn't have visitors? I have... multiple times.

We had so many late term fetal demises for moms who had COVID.

Before the morgue trucks I got to lay a dead 38 week infant on top of someone who had died from COVID in the icu because we had run out of spaces in our morgue. No one ever wants to hear those stories.

The daughter who spent every night ugly crying at her mom's bedside in the ICU. Daughter was diagnosed with COVID, didn't believe it was real, and went to her parents house for Christmas. Mom and dad both get COVID and wind up in the ICU. Last I saw, dad was on heated high flow and getting ready to go to step down. Mom was intubated, vented, maxed out on oxygen and struggling to maintain her saturation in the 60% range. I worked nights. Every night I worked she was there, ugly crying and wailing.

The guy who needed the whole ICU team and the intensivist to turn him on his belly because he was COVID positive and unstable. Maybe he'll make it 20 minutes before having to be flipped back over.

Those two cases will stay with me for life.

I had a patient who was a denier. This was in late 2021. Intubated him and his last words were it shouldn't be possible for COVID to be this severe and serious. He should not be sick with it. He was 35, fit etc. He died. Because he didn't mask and didn't believe it was real. When we literally lived next to the first major epicenter of COVID in the US. After all we had been through the year before…

I'm horrified at all these stories I read saying they had Tyvek suits and full head respirators and all this gear. Where was that stuff for my hospital? We had old school yellow rain slickers, reused N-95's that didn't even fit after being worn for hours and "sanitized," those godawful food service gloves that leak and are tissue paper thin, sanitizer from a distillery that I'm pretty sure was actually just vodka with a glug of floor cleaner. At one point, we got a batch of gloves that 1/3 the staff were allergic to, and people had rashes up to their elbows for weeks.

Patients turning grape juice purple from hypoxia on hi-flow oxygen with a non-rebreather on top of that. The absolute backbreaking work of trying to clean and change 200lb+ patients who couldn't tolerate being anything but vertical, couldn't put out any effort, and would get aggressive after 20 seconds as hypoxia and panic set in. Being soaked to the skin with sweat and shivering when you go to change gowns before the next room. People begging us to let them die/crying for us to save them in every room. Calling a death notification and realizing it's the third or fourth time you've called this particular person/family.

I live 5 blocks from LifeCare center in Kirkland, Washington… yes, the very first hot spot where two thirds of the patients and staff got ill or died in two weeks. 47 sick, 35 dead. I knew something bad was going to happen when we got the first case in Everett (I think January 18th or so; he came back from China on the 15th). That patient was not contained. Later we would learn that he was in contact with several people, and of those some visited LifeCare Center. Shit accelerated here on February 28th. New case confirmed at LCC… Feb 29th state of emergency declared by the governor. Suddenly, the world slowed down… I knew what was coming. My niece is an ICU nurse in Paris and they were getting swamped with cases (her ICU had basically been collecting all the COVID cases in France since mid January). Then people started dying at LCC. A lot of people.

On March 1st, my neighborhood started getting a lot of ambulance activity… but it was just LCC descending into the hellfire pit. My husband decided to stay home from work (he is immunocompromised). By March 4th, things were getting weirder; more silent now, but for the incessant back and forth of medical helicopters above my house…

Evergreen was filled to the brim with dying people from the care center in no time. Then every ICU around the area got filled. The Kirkland Fire department had so many direct exposures that by March 3rd, 19 firefighters were sick. The neighborhood was getting cordoned off; public health official stuff was happening (extra help maybe, emergency cell; I can't remember).

I worked at UWMC in the post anesthesia care unit… and found out the virology lab had now tested several positive.

March 4th. Families are getting mad because they can't see their loved ones. No info is given, etc. They call a press conference.

March 6th. The FEDERAL crisis disaster unit comes. The governor makes a public announcement, asking people to limit visits etc. I know that means we are going down.

We are getting the first COVID cases in my hospital.

More press conferences. Cancelling Girl Scout cookie season is being seriously discussed by parents. I know it's weird to think about this, but my daughter was selling...

My hospital is starting to ask nurses what they are comfortable with, and process more N95s. Purrell starts to disappear from rooms and hallways (people are taking it home with them...)

My colleagues in the ICUs nearby are saying it is bad. That COVID patients are some of the worst patients they have ever seen. They are using a lot of PPE, and it starting to feel like that we are not going to see a decrease in numbers soon. How right were they...

March 13th. Cookie season is officially stopped early (before closing weekend). My hospital is preparing for crap to really hit the fan. Canceling elective surgeries. Limiting visitors. On the 15th, stay home is recommended. The governor issues a mandatory stay home order on the 22 or 23. But only essential workers are okay to be out. And my hospital is now doing zero surgeries unless it's an emergency or life saving necessity. Since I work in the PACU, we are asked if we want to float to ICU.

A whole unit is transformed into an ICU and literally walled off from the hospital. All nurses are asked to list all their skills, especially ICU/CCU, ventilator care, ECMO and other cardiac assistance equipment. I used to do ECMO. But it has been a decade at least. Everybody is getting nose swabbed up the wazoo. We are getting exposed to patients turning positive after they were negative before surgery. I have colleagues in other facilities saying they are reusing N95 masks and gowns. I float to ICU. It is full. All the time. We are managing vent allocation like it's the rarest commodity. The toll is climbing. People outside have no idea how horrendous this is. Sedation sometimes doesn't work. Sometimes we don't have enough. Awake intubated patients suffering. Already, some are denying that COVID is real. One of the docs I know in another faculty gets COVID from being at the bedside. He is admitted in his own unit. Patients are mobilizing 1:1, hell, even 3:1, and nurses don't have enough arms to do all the work, and we are getting short staffed, and we are getting sick. I go float when I can. Because elective surgeries are stopped, we are getting sent home because of low census, and a furlough is apparently on the table.

The two weeks of mandatory stay home order turn into months. Patients are getting sicker and more are coming.

And then PPE is rationed. Already in April .

And the spiraling in Dante's inferno was only beginning...

N95 were getting names on them, one per shift. Then for the week. And then one in as long as 5 weeks...

I remember being EKG tech and staffing the hospital 24/7 so RT wouldn't have to worry about overnight EKGs and we also staffed the ER so EMTs didn't have to worry about it between two hospitals. At the hospital on the affluent part of town one of the nurses was complaining that COVID was a hoax because she hadn't seen anyone with COVID there. The ER provider and I were livid because we'd worked the same shift for a while and I kept ending up at the same hospitals and when we worked the hospital that was centrally located we were always busy with COVID patients. The centrally located hospital had already filled up and they were using a part of the ER for holding because rooms weren't opening up upstairs. The centrally located hospital was also closer for all of the people in our community who worked front line jobs, so they were hit the hardest compared to the affluent end in the beginning where they could all work remotely.

I remember weekly schedules, being floated to the COVID unit to be an on-site tele tech, the interpreters on a stick/the phone being unable to hear the patient because of how much oxygen they were on and it was so loud. I remember patients in ICU who weren't intubated communicating on paper through the glass door to their loved ones because their loved one couldn't hear them on the phone with the noise from the oxygen. I remember wishing I could do more as a tech because the nurses, respiratory therapists, and providers were being run ragged.

Working in a birthing unit, there was so much uncertainty around how to best protect newborns born to COVID positive mothers that the initial policy was to separate them at birth and keep the babies in incubators for 2 weeks in the NICU. We just didn't know. It took ~1-2 months of reassuring data before we could keep those babies in room with their mothers.

It haunts me how many 12-hr shifts I spent in isolation rooms with perfectly healthy babies in incubators, limiting contact to care times every 3 hrs, per protocol. Every time I took a baby out, I was terrified I'd cross-contaminate something and get them sick. It was awful to not have enough information at the time, but it's somehow worse now knowing the separation wasn't necessary.

I worked in the OR of a relatively busy Level 1 trauma center. My unit wasn't especially impacted at first, then they shut down elective surgeries. Many of us were floated to other units, a skeleton crew was kept on to handle urgent and emergent surgeries.

It went on like this for a couple of months, and then the governor declared that everything was reopening, including elective surgeries. And then we were told we would no longer be cancelling elective COVID+ cases. Within a month of this decision, we had such a large cluster among staff that the CDC and local health department came to investigate.

I remember the day I first had symptoms. I called in to work and was told 14 other people had also called in with COVID symptoms. Over the next few days 20 or so more came up positive. The OR had to be shut down again except for emergent cases.

For most of the staff, they did their 10-day quarantine and came back with only a few lingering issues. Not so for me. Five days after I was diagnosed, my wife had to take me to the ED because I couldn't breathe. I will never forget having to say goodbye to my wife in the parking lot and walk myself in because they wouldn't allow her into the department. I honestly didn't know at the time if I was saying goodbye for the last time.

I was admitted with COVID pneumonia, and spent a very tough nearly 3 weeks in the hospital. I never had to be intubated, thankfully, but it was a close call, and I had that conversation with my pulmonologist, who happened to ve someone I also worked closely with in the OR. There was a hurricane coming, and my wife was quarantining at home alone because she had also tested positive, though thankfully her symptoms were mild. We were lucky that the hurricane turned at the last minute and missed us, but I was so worried for my wife.

I think what I remember the most is being so tired, but afraid to go to sleep because I might not wake up again. When I was finally released I was still in pretty bad shape, and spent most of the next month on supplemental oxygen. Now almost 5 years later I continue to have problems that I can directly trace back to COVID.

I'll never forget the times I was coding a patient with another nurse in a room in our space suits while the doctor, respiratory therapist, and even the pharmacist were yelling all the orders through the glass wall. It was difficult to hear in those respirator suits, so they'd write on the glass wall and I'd have to read backwards while bagging the patient. No one would enter the room. We were disposable. The entire staff of the hospital wouldn't come near the COVID unit where I worked. Trash piled up. There were fruit flies and smelly soiled laundry bags everywhere. "Fine for thee, but not for me". Every clinic nurse, administrator, educator, and those in "leadership roles" stayed home for the whole pandemic. Fully paid. Not a single one volunteered for even one hour to assist us in the ER (while we were all getting sick because the rooms were incorrectly sealed/ventilated.) My previously healthy 46-year-old coworker has permanent lung damage, has been stented twice and has valve issues due to getting COVID several times. It was traumatizing. Clinics answered phone calls and sent EVERYONE to the ER for any need, emergent or not. I was angry and disappointed in my fellow nurses and clinicians who wouldn't dare consider helping us while knowing we were struggling. It feels like a moral injury.

I took care of a talking head during the Delta surge. If you're semi-politically aware of political talk show personalities then you know who this person is, or at least you've heard of them in passing as a B-Lister. He cried. He was terrified he was going to die. And he came pretty close to doing so. Never was in the ICU but was in our COVID unit. But he didn't. Now he gets to tell everyone that COVID was a hoax and Fauci needs to be prosecuted. He's never mentioned anywhere I can tell he even had COVID.

Chicago. It was like nothing I have ever seen in my 20 plus years respiratory therapy career in the ICU/ER. Watched while we worked a code on an 18-year old for two hours; died. So much more. Space suits. We were together a year, all of us in COVID. It was weird how the staff never changed. Even though we were 7 days a week, 13 hours a day. It's cliche to say, but my coworkers, in COVID, we became family. I know everything about you and you know everything about me and round and round we go.

My story is a little different, since I worked on a med-surg oncology floor. We were the only unit in the hospital that couldn't have COVID patients because it could wipe out our immunocompromised patients.

Because of that we got absolutely dumped on. Every confused, violent patient got sent to us, as long as they were COVID negative and the hospital needed a COVID bed empty. We each always had 6 patients to watch, and were lucky to have 2 CNAs on a 36 bed floor. I get it, the other units needed beds empty, but that didn't help when we were getting donkey kicked or punched at.

We got loads of patients that should NEVER have come to a med surg floor but since they weren't vented, they'd throw them in a med-surg bed, where we would frequently have to rapid/code them later when they did crash. We went from a unit that rarely had codes (cancer patients usually see the writing on the wall before the time comes and go comfort measures only) to having one every day. Every day we got more and more acute patients, more and more we would get harassed because our metrics were bad, our fall numbers were up, didn't fill out some specific piece of paper for our skin audits. But admin didn't give a fuck we had 6 medically complex fresh post operation patients with one CNA for 36 rooms. My manager literally told me "staffing isn't an excuse for falls" (????)

I also remember constantly dealing with abusive family members mad about the visitation policy. and our administration didn't give a fuck because if the family member bitched enough admin would let them the fuck on in anyway and then we'd look like the assholes for enforcing the rules. or people calling saying "well so-and-so gave us an exception." Like, bitch, I don't know who that is.

I also remember a man who was a COVID patient (but was now negative). COVID had basically turned him into a vegetable, he was in for secondary pneumonia and slowly dying. He was a ward of the state, and we could not get ahold of his rep at the DHHR so we had to continue to treat him for weeks until they eventually made him "do not resuscitate". He was so far gone by that point he didn't have a blink reflex, and his eyes turned black before he died from drying out.

Appalachia here. We ran out of PPE pretty quickly. I bought a painter's respirator and P100/P95 cartridges early on. Got made fun of for a while, until everyone else was reusing N95s for weeks. We were wearing trash bag ponchos and tyvek painting suits for a while.

I had a surreal night shift where we carted out so many bodies that the funeral homes were full. We brought one into the biggest home in the county. The director and his partner had been running the crematorium in shifts around the clock. He looked as tired as we felt, and directed us to a refrigerated truck that was idling in the back lot. It had the Wendy's logo on the side; the local emergency management had commandeered it from the company. Grandmas and Grandpas stacked like cordwood. Once they were full we got sent to the small mom and pop funeral home across the county. They didn't have any refrigeration and were already working on one on the table. That director was stopping for a beer in the middle of work. We put that grandpa in the viewing room after clearing empty beer cans off the table. A week later I got added to a group chat by my wife's birth father where his idiot friends wanted to gossip about how COVID wasn't real.

When COVID first started everyone was scared. My contractor didn't want to work on my house anymore since I worked at the hospital. There was no cure or treatment or vaccine and people were terrified. He's now MAGA anti-vax. Why? My guess is because of the mandatory lockdowns and enforcement of rules. As a smart, intelligent person I understood why it was important, but it was too hard to educate the masses. So instead, the government just shut everything down and told people what to do. And people do not like their autonomy taken away, so they rebelled against everything and created their own mindset and false reality. Eventually, they forgot the fear they once had. Replacing it with anger and alternative facts that made them feel they had a sense of control.

I very much remember working at a long term care facility and a very kind male patient mouthing at me (because he didn't have the breath to speak) "Please let me die." He declined to be intubated. I'll never forget watching him struggle for breath.

I remember seeing my first x-ray whited out with fibrosis and having nightmares about it for months.

I remember the breakdown and sores on my face from the mask. I also remember being confused by Zoom because none of my work could be done remotely. I felt very much like I inhabited an entirely separate world from everyone else.

I remember contracting COVID for the first time, gasping in my bed with pneumonia and wondering if I would die on a vent like so many of my patients.

The one thing I miss and appreciated about COVID was I never had to see a single c-suite asshole in the emergency department the entire pandemic. Usually they'd come parade through; mostly on day shift, but every once and awhile on a night shift. Strut around, look self important, that sort of thing. But not during COVID. Not during the worst of it. Not when we had 12-15 hour wait times. I never saw any of them. That's really how we could track when the worst of the pandemic was over, was when they started coming back. "Nature is healing", right. They were fine with us going into the fray with garbage bags as PPE but it was too much to ask for them to be seen on the floor.

https://drive.google.com/file/d/1IpTaKcIHUpAXDyiKvaqjTLofs4n OjIlS/view?usp=sharing

62 year old anti-vaxxer, family was refusing to vax "in solidarity" with her. She refused to believe she had COVID. Mirco-emboli in face while we were laying her prone. Three quarters of her face was just dead, necrotic tissue. She did eventually pass. Would've needed a face transplant if she survived.

He was an older gentleman, early 70s, fully vaxxed, lung cancer diagnosis. He was undergoing chemo and radiation. Apparently the radiation burns to his esophagus made it difficult to swallow. I don't really know, I didn't have the pleasure of having him early on. He was admitted to ICU, I guess, because they thought he'd do poorly. He only remained on a bit of O2, but ended up in atrial fibrillation. He was eventually transferred to a medical-surgical unit to admit sicker people. Somewhere along the way, he got worse. I was told it was a mix of anxiety and COVID. He wasn't breathing well, and he knew it. He kept telling his nurse that night "thank you, you're saving my life".

The hospitalists arrived that morning to see him and immediately moved my COVID positive, DKA patient to admit him. He was placed on a positive pressure mask. Then he was intubated that afternoon. When I came back to work, the first thing I saw was a big basket of snacks at the nurses station.

"Is this for us?"

"No, it's for ICU Room 4."

Apparently he's a snacker.

I entered his room to find bags of snacks, and a Reese's of some sort on his bedside table. Probably from when he was actually conscious and could eat it. My stomach growled. I haven't eaten all day. I'm one of those assholes who doesn't eat and loses weight when they're stressed. I've lost 10 lbs since transferring to this unit.

My coworker and I spend hours getting our 2-4 intubated patients in acceptable condition. Why didn't dayshift put a glide sheet under him so we could move him? There is blood on the floor from his arterial line. I know they were busy and did their best, but my OCD heart is pissed.

Hours pass. Drips are hung constantly. Levophed is keeping this man's blood pressure high enough to be alive. I'm dealing with incompetent residents, who I expect to know more than I do, to help me. At one point, I slow push (against my best judgment) a dose of labetalol through his IV, per order the doctor's order, for my patient's heart rate. It bottoms out his blood pressure immediately, and I max out his Levophed. I spend a scary half an hour at his bedside, patient in Trendelenburg (feet in the air, head to the ground), praying for his blood pressure to come up. He is a full code. I don't cry.

I message the on-call doctor about what happened. How could this go wrong? I trusted him. I gave him every detail so that he would be well informed. He was wrong, and my patient suffered.

Somehow we make it. I have 36 hours off.

I come back to find my patient is a Do Not Resuscitate. His wife and son were allowed to visit. They made the correct and difficult decision. He remains intubated, breathing tube down his throat, but what will happen will happen. His blood pressure is dropping. We turn his blood pressure medications, his Levophed and Vasopressin, up as high as we can. His heart rate spikes. I'm delaying the inevitable.

I have a medical/surgical nurse with me, floated to the help us in the ICU. Somehow, their floor only has a few patients and she is training to take an intermediate load. I've only been here less than a year, and I tell her this; she still chooses me to train with. None of what I'm doing is what she needs to see, but she was with this patient when he went bad on the floor. She knows him better than I do.

She quickly learns how exhausting it is to keep up with his drips. Levophed, Vasopressin, Fentanyl, Propofol: at any given point, something is being changed out or adjusted. God forbid you don't have that Levo scanned and ready at the bedside. His life is in that bag.

We're doing our due diligence, but his heart rate sucks. I'm suctioning foamy secretions every hour. Urine output is nil. Gastric contents are positive for blood. I'm battling a fever unrelieved by Tylenol and cooling efforts.

Around 0530, I go into the room alone. My orientee is exhausted. I don't blame her. I know that feeling. It could be due to my poor planning and time management. We've been in his room every hour for at least a half hour. It can be like that sometimes, but I'm especially awful at this, I feel. I do my 0600 duties: empty a negligible amount of urine, empty gastric contents, turn, care to make sure he doesn't get pneumonia from the ventilator, make sure everything in the room is replenished and the way I'd like to see it before day shift comes on. Take the trash out because housekeeping just won't do it overnight in COVID rooms. Breathe a sigh of relief as I close the sliding doors. Maybe I've made it to 0705.

I wash my hands and notice his rhythm has changed. What was once atrial fibrillation in the 120s-130s, is now a wide ventricular rhythm in the 60s. I tell everybody around that things are changing, but no one listens. Earbuds are plugged in. We are coasting until shift change. I busy myself with restocking until I can't look away from the monitor. It happened quicker than I thought. I gown up and hold his hand until his heart stops. And that's it. He's gone. 0558. House supervisor comes up to confirm. 0608, but I know when it really happened. She handles the phone calls, which I'm not used to. My orientee and I remove all his leads and catheters and clean up. Most of this is new to us. Will the arterial line or PICC line bleed much? The arterial doesn't, the PICC does. I clean up his final shit. Everyone was so worried about his constipation.

Putting someone in a body bag is so fucking unceremonious. I don't care what you say about dying with dignity. Put someone in a fucking body bag. They are just meat and flesh and weight. I open the window for him.

I came home in a mood. I swore I wouldn't keep doing this. I make breakfast for my husband, silently willing him to work quicker. I shower, and when he's gone, I take a long, hard pull from the bottle of tequila I have hidden in the freezer. I can't keep doing this.

I don't cry.

I was a Med Lab Tech who directly worked in the department that did the hospital testing. It's a side no one really hears from.

There was a national shortage on the lab supplies needed to do the testing. Masks were being validated for reuse after being autoclaved to make sure they still worked. My lab was initially denied N95 Masks while they were given to pathology residents until we went to our union rep and pointed out how we were directly handling the samples. In my lab, we ended up training these same residents on decades-old manual methods of nucleic acid extraction since supplies were so low early on, with varying results. But, it helped, and I am grateful for their hard work.

The CDC test was WRONG. The primer designs sucked and the controls were invalid. Best bet was to use the WHO version. As time went by, companies scrambled to make their own tests. Those have to be fully validated before we can use them for testing. That takes time and effort away from the sheer volume of testing. As an aside, about six months before this hit the fan, the CDC was instructed by the Trump Administration to not use words like "evidence-based" and "science" in their documents for the public. There had also been a massive brain drain. Fast forward to the pandemic, they initially couldn't decide if masks were necessary... for a respiratory disease.

Yeah.

The morgue and grieving room happened to be near our lab. For the family that was allowed in, you could hear the wailing daily for hours on end. The rest you see crying in the parking lot. Residents were afraid to do autopsies on COVID patients because they weren't sure if they were properly protected. Can't blame them.

I will end with this: it was already here for months before the government cared. In the lab, we always tested for respiratory viruses, including the flu. However, the tests only pick up known things. Nurses and doctors were asking more and more for repeats on samples that were completely negative because their patients were clearly suffering. Their bacterial cultures were negative. Both the labs and the nurses were checking sample collection was correct, verifying our reagents were good, and the machines weren't glitching out. They were all fine, but tests were showing nothing. Because it was SARS-CoV2...and we were never alerted until our state department of health sounded the alarm way before the CDC did.

My final thoughts for the time: I lived in one of the earliest hard hit areas in the US. We have a very dense network of hospital and medical centers. I recall remarking to my colleagues: "I hope the middle part of the country is getting prepared, because if we are overwhelmed with all our hospitals, they will be utterly screwed."

They didn't. They were.

I was in the cath lab as a unit supervisor when it broke out.

They started floating us nurses to the unit, and then started floating my RTs as well since we had cancelled elective cases.

In the early days I felt like we were winging it a little bit, and of course we were always short on PPE.

Then one of my RTs that got floated to the unit to act as a CNA came down with COVID. He was dead inside of a week.

That was a hellish time to be in healthcare. Administration threw us to the wolves, with raw steak hung around our necks.

Those pieces of trash were sitting at home counting bonus money while we were ground under. Mandatory OT. Shifts pushed at times to 16 hours.

That shit broke me.

Leaving bedside nursing was the best thing I ever did for myself, but I still deal with carried trauma from it.

I go out of my way to discourage anyone from going into the profession if I am asked about it.

Not a COVID vet, but during COVID I had a fall in my mom's attic (this was three hours from home) and broke four ribs and bruised my kidney. I initially had blood in my urine. I went to the ER for this. The normal practice would have been to put me in a hospital room for two days of observation, to make sure that I would get immediate care if my kidney did rupture, which is a life threatening situation. In fact, I had orders to be put in a hospital room when one was available. None was, because the hospital was full of COVID patients. They were on gurneys lining the walls of the corridors in the ER. I ended up spending 36 or so hours in an ER bed, with five other patients in an ER room. When they discovered I could walk and when there was no blood in my urine, they sent me home, but directed me to see my PCP ASAP. I saw her the next day, and she ordered another scan. A few hours later when the results came back, she called me at home and told me to rush to my local ER, as my scans were alarming her. Went to the local ER, and since there was no blood in my urine and no available hospital rooms, they sent me home again. Thankfully the kidney never ruptured, but I could easily have been one of those excess deaths indirectly caused by COVID.

When I was a resident in 2020, I watched people die everyday in the ICU for months. No effective treatment, multiorgan failure from clots everywhere, intubated, lined up, slowly died. This repeated for months, countless faces, so many phone calls to loved ones with the news. All the while worrying I might contract COVID. When the vaccine came out in December I was so relieved to get it.

I looked at the "Airborne Precautions" sign on the wall and as I was donning my PPE to enter room eighteen, I looked through the glass door at my patient then his monitor. He was pale, diaphoretic, and using his abdominal muscles to breathe. The vital signs monitor bell alarmed and I saw his oxygen saturation at 75%. I entered the room and introduced myself, "Hi! My name is Hana; I am going to be your nurse today" while simultaneously placing a non-rebreather with 15 liters of oxygen over his face. My patient nodded. I cracked open the door to his room and asked a nurse who was walking by to call both respiratory therapy and the physician, and then turned back to face my patient. He was shivering but the thermometer reading showed that he did not have a fever. "Are you scared?" I asked. He nodded back in response. I told him that he was in the right place and that I'd do my best to help him.

After some time passed, I entered his room. The respiratory therapist placed a high-flow nasal cannula and his oxygen saturation improved to 89%, but he was still working to breathe. I was about to leave his room to get medication for my other patient when he asked, "Can you stay for a second?". I didn't have much time, but I pulled up a rolling chair and listened. He was initially frustrated, and did not believe that COVID was real or that his swab tested positive for the virus. "I must have the flu," he insisted. It was easy to recognize his denial. When I didn't argue with him, the conversation then shifted to reflection. The man opened the pictures on his phone and showed his grandchildren. He told me each of their names and of their developing personalities. "I need to make it out of this hospital to see them again," he said. I squeezed his hand in response. I couldn't reassure him honestly; I knew his prognosis was poor after seeing the CT scan of his lungs..

At the end of my shift, I opened his room one last time to say goodbye. "Thank you for being there," he said, behind the hissing of his CPAP mask that he had been upgraded to. Putting myself in this patient's shoes, I realized how frightening it must have been hearing the monitor alarms and being alone in an unfamiliar environment and struggling to breathe.

He was one of hundreds of COVID patients I cared for during the pandemic.

At my skilled nursing facility, I volunteered to work the COVID unit (about 60 patients) as unlike others, I didn't have kids. I didn't work there much (as others wanted the double pay), but one day there were only 2 of us nurses in the entire unit. We sent out ten patients that eight hours shift (each about 5), and you knew they weren't going to come back. All we could do is just try to take care of 30 patients, and it seemed like around at least 4-6 of them were terrified that they couldn't breathe, all the while you are dripping in sweat from wearing a plastic laundry bag.

My director of nursing was one of the first to get it in our building. Got flu and COVID at the same time. Was on a respirator for 4 weeks and thankfully managed to pull through. It took her 3 months to talk again, and then she retired a few months after she came back. That was the good news.

Had a husband and wife on the skilled floor (not COVID). The husband had severe COPD and I just kept on saying "Get him the f*** out here!" But they said, in his condition, there wasn't a way to get him home (true but better than dying). Just a really nice guy. Found out he died after I came back from COVID, I was his nurse most days, so I probably gave it to him. I still regret not pushing hard enough to get him out.

My absolute favorite patient was this one lady who was 101 years old. Had dementia but rolled around the place and went wherever she wanted to go and was the nicest/funniest resident. She'd always hang at our nurse's station when we were charting. Any time we had a work pizza-ish party she was there.

She got COVID, but it didn't kill her. She didn't have to go to the hospital. It took her mind away. She spent her final 3 months in bed, not saying a word. And yes, she was 101 years old, but it just hurt going into that room and seeing her final days; not eating, not talking, and not drinking.

I remember one day, early on, we'd just implemented surveillance - if a test had been performed on a household and they were quarantining, it would pop up on our mobile data terminal, and we got called out to a CPR in progress on a 40-something year old woman. She had been tested, her daughter (20) had been tested too. Both sick. We were still prohibited from using nebulizers, intubation had changed, there were strict field termination criteria - we couldn't use heroic effort anymore. We pulled up, started getting on our PPE, getting all of our equipment, and the 20 year old daughter comes out of the house and starts screaming at us -- my mama, my mama, she's dead what the fuck are yall doing? Yall just out here standing here, she's dead, she's dead. She starts shoving us and getting physical and I look up at this cop who's a block away, watching, who hand gestures to us like, "you good?" ...and I'm like... no. I'm not. But it's obvious Captain Copper wasn't gonna come help us, so our supervisor became our daughter wrangler and we went inside. She was a field termination, she had passed probably earlier the night before, while the daughter slept through her COVID haze. I remember her screaming and trying to yank our PPE off. The supervisor just physically holding her, all the firefighters clearing off the scene, nobody wanted to go near this whole mess so we were just left to swim through alone and figure it out. Try to comfort her as best we could, but what can you say, you know? Yelling through a mask on some hot tropical morning, trying to be kind but you just come off condescending.

I remember the cops not wanting to go into nursing homes or assisted living, any communal living spaces. We had this one sudden death and they asked me if it looked suspicious or if they were needed and I was like, "I don't fuckin' know, man?" And it really dawned on me that this was their line. This was it.

I remember one guy... young, too. He was my age. Like... 30. COVID positive. He'd just gotten back from a flight. In the delta wave. He also met field termination criteria because he was too far gone. I wanted to work him anyway. My supervisor told me to clear up because we already had another. She was yelling at me from the doorway; didn't want to put on her PPE if she didn't have to. I remember his girlfriend crying and crying, "He can't leave me! He can't leave me, we just had a baby, no, he can't leave me!" I wanted so badly to help her. To stay. To... fix it, but his body temp was already in the 80s in a room temperature room. Rules were rules, and I had no latitude.

Then there was this one guy, early days... he said he just felt like he had a cold, but wanted to go to the hospital. I told him, naw man, you don't, they're gonna test you for COVID and put you in iso and you don't wanna deal with all that, he was insistent. He was worried because he had hypertension. And I was like, fuck it, and we took him in, and I got there, and it was my first real transport in the early days for something like this to this one particular facility, and I was like... uncertain how things would go, cause I assumed procedures would be different, but I had no firsthand experience. I'd only seen the movies, you know? We'd called it in, we rolled up, and there was plastic sheeting they'd taped up everywhere, and they told me to move him to a wheelchair and come bring him into the antechamber and then leave. No real report; it felt... dystopian. Like a horror movie. He gets cold feet, starts yelling at me to not let them take him back there, he changed his mind, and I had this moment where I realized that nobody else knew how this stuff was supposed to go either. We all just had movies and tropes and all these weird silly things in our head, at every level, and we were all just trying our best but nobody knew what to actually do. I got back in the truck, told my partner we couldn't take people to the ER anymore. She asked what we were going to do. I said I didn't know. (I wound up calling a lot of PCPs, doing treat-in-place orders, and doing refusals on people against their will. If they were truly urgent, I took them. But most clinic-esque things we just consulted their doc. I wound up with some real creative solutions.)

I asked a friend in New York, what was the first one where he really knew. He recounted a patient that he had who looked fine with a pulse oxygenation in the 30% range. My first one, I can still smell her house. Still see her. I knew her, knew her family. Knew her son, who was a type one diabetic. Thought we were going out for him, just some sugar and on our way. It was her. She just felt weak. Pulse ox in the 20s. I felt my heart sink. I remember him asking if she'd be ok. I knew him, he knew me. I know I didn't hide it on my face very well. He asked if she had it, I said yes. He said, well, they have to test, and- and I said, "No. She has it." He kept... looking for these assurances I couldn't give him. I knew she'd probably never come back home. I watched them intubate her in the ER.

I hope he got to say goodbye.

I'm a nurse who worked in the ER through COVID and beyond. I spent 12 hours one shift in a section of the department that had 3 curtained rooms and two rooms with doors. All 5 patients were COVID positive, some on ventilators, some on high flow oxygen. The doctor asked me via a walkie talkie from outside the closed doors of the area if I thought one of the patients needed to be intubated.

"How about you come in here and assess your patient?"

"No," he said. "I need to limit my exposure."

We were offered the vaccine fairly early on. My partner and I got it before our final shift on our day four rotation. We both shared a few quiet tears. It felt like the fog was finally about to lift. Everyone at our company was offered the shot including dispatchers. Most took the opportunity. This was early enough that only some of the public had access to the vaccine but most healthcare workers were receiving it and it was only going to get more available. It's not like they were taking it from someone.

One of our dispatchers refused the vaccine. He didn't politely and quietly decline. He was extremely vocal about how it wasn't safe and he didn't want any part of it. I didn't know him except in passing so I wasn't aware of this until he got sick. He was admitted to the COVID floor of one of our hospitals. He was eventually intubated.

He spent multiple weeks on a ventilator slowly declining. I don't remember how long it took exactly as that entire year has been blurred together, but I do remember thinking that he lasted much longer than most did.

Because he was at one of our regular hospitals and because we were all reaching for something his family brought in some walkie talkies. They were some shitty off brand set but they worked enough to go from the EMS break room to his room upstairs.

Whenever we transported a patient to that ED we would stop by the EMS room that was really just a bathroom and a microwave. Sometimes you'd get lucky and there would be popsicles in the normally empty mini fridge. We would queue up the mic and talk. No one ever talked back.

Since I didn't know him I usually stuck with standard radio traffic. "Medic 300 is transport complete" some would tell him to get better or that we were thinking of him. I remember walking past that room and seeing someone talking to him with tears rolling down their face. I skipped the microwave and ate my lunch cold that day.

I think we all invented new stages of grief during that time. Some days I would see that walkie talkie and want to sob. Some days I would be so angry. I thought about all the nurses upstairs who were in a different world than us but fighting in the same direction. I thought about how they were fighting to keep this guy alive when he had chosen this. I thought about how we were randomly interrupting their day while they were drowning in layers of used PPE and trying to fix IVs through fogged up face shields. I wondered if they minded hearing us. I wondered if they hated us a little bit. I thought they would blame us. I probably would have.

I thought about talking to the other people in the room. The nurses or techs or doctors who maybe hated us. I wanted to say thank you or sorry or somehow say that the world was still turning outside of the prison they were locked in for 12 hours a day. I never figured out how to say any of that. I'm still unsure how to explain most of that year and our thousand stages of grief.

Eventually or finally he died. I suspect that his room was immediately filled by someone else in the same situation. It probably stayed that way for a year at least.

I've read a hundred accounts of what people went through then. I've tried to explain to those who worked from home what it feels like to do CPR in a tyvec suit that gets go hot you feel nauseous and lightheaded. When people ask me what it was like I think about that stupid walkie talkie that never talked back. I still don't really know how to explain that.

I never thought I'd see so much death so quickly. A lady so hypoxic she was actually purple on 100% high-flow nasal cannula oxygen gasp-screamed at me "I DON'T BELIEVE IN COVID"

I worked ICU at a smaller community hospital. During the worst COVID spikes we would have a ratio at times of about 3/4 COVID patients in the hospital and 1/4 regular patients. Surgeries were suspended unless emergent. People were so sick, nothing we did helped. I had never seen anything close to it with other viruses causing pneumonia. A few went into DIC and there were many blood clotting issues. Mostly respiratory failure eventually leading to other body systems shutting down. We had to use high flow/ positive pressure to keep them alive with many sustaining positive pressure injuries. Many coded during intubation and if they survived, died on the vent. I was in many people's room when they died when it should have been family with them. Short staffing hit and I had 7 COVID patients at once during a spike which was absolutely terrible and unsafe. Through the pandemic and especially during the Delta wave, vaccinated people were not my patients. They didn't get that sick with it. My patients were all unvaxxed except 2 that had cancer or other immunosuppressive diseases. The horrible things I witnessed people go through due to the virus who were well with maybe only a few prior managed comorbidities a couple of weeks earlier will never leave me. The grief will never leave me completely. I won't forget and I won't work another pandemic no matter the compensation. I'm finally working through the anxiety disorder that I attribute to working the pandemic that I didn't have before and have been doing well for 9 months. I'll never forget the names of the people I cared for and I'm still so sorry for what happened to them.

I got shielded from a lot of the worst of COVID from working air medical, but we got the gamut. April of 21, dispatched for a FEMA evacuation of Jamaica Hospital in NYC. "Find this patient, transport them to that hospital". Full PPE, acclimating to the spring warmth so overheating on the ambulance ride to and from the airport and during the hospital transitions of care. The patient you were going to get usually wasn't by the door, and the rooms were jam packed with people so that you were crawling over them to find the patient, then dragging yours over top of all the other ones to get them out of the room. Sometimes the patient you were after was long dead. And plenty of other times, a different patient you had to crawl over was long dead. Back and forth, all day and all night. The pilots were able to swap out for their mandatory service time, but the crews kept hauling.

On the flip side, country kids had a mixed bag. I flew at least 2 major abuse cases per month from parents not being able to go to work, the stresses of not being able to keep up with bills, and the access to alcohol or other more illicit substances that created a perfect storm for child abuse. I also was able to directly observe a correlating uptick in flights for patients that were subject to spousal abuse. A small rise in shootings, a couple more stabbings, but a bunch more beatings. Other traumas also rose-the number of kids that we flew due to ATV accidents or bicycle versus motor vehicle kept us busy for a full year, and helped sustain some of our other bases that weren't seeing the upticks in COVID transports. These kids weren't entirely to blame; they were just kids being kids that were out of school, had poor access to education platforms due to the schools being unprepared for a sudden transition to online learning combined with an internet infrastructure that couldn't support the platforms well anyways, and parents that if they were fortunate were at work. So a 10 or 12 year old that normally would have been chaperoned was seeing a beautiful spring day, had nothing to do and no one to tell them how to do it, and took an ATV that they were unsuited to operate out in the fields and roads. Some were pretty benign, some major.

And the distrust. Even though I'm as backwoods as my neighbors, they couldn't bring themselves to believe that things were as bad in the big cities as I was telling them-and continued to be incredulous when the local places filled up. Politicians on both sides decrying their opposition and grandstanding, then flip flopping their positions and grandstanding the opposite of what they had before. My inlaws being disgusted with me for masking up to do the assessments they asked me to come do once they'd been diagnosed. My cousins mocking me for saying that they were idiots for not getting the vaccine and not believing when I said Trump was the one pushing people to get it, not just the Democrats-and simultaneously saying it was the sickest they'd ever been and that they were surprised they lived when they *did* catch COVID, but that it wasn't as bad as they'd been led to believe by the media. And that while the hospital was full to the point of beds in the inpatient hallways, "it didn't seem that busy". But not to give any credit to the left either-they said at the beginning it was just the Republicans fear mongering and being xenophobic, then shutting everything down to punish the left-leaning cities for wanting to remain open. And then not understanding the outcry when people couldn't pay their bills because they weren't working when the Democrats were wanting to keep the lockdowns and various mandates going.

And the internal healthcare debacle. Private citizens buying up all the PPE they could and hoarding it when hospitals and EMS weren't able to obtain any. The FEMA stockpile being so dry rotted that it literally fell apart in your hands. Hospitals locking it up and threatening legal charges against staff that got their own. Hospitals cutting staff loose, only to clamor for staff as the waves hit. Rationing ventilators, rationing sedation meds FEMA ventilators that weren't up to the task of maintaining most regular patients-let alone COVID patients. The ever-changing guidance on cohorting, PPE, treatments, when to intubate versus maintain...

When COVID started, I was working inpatient Peds mental health. We had jack shit for PPE. Outbreaks kept happening because the majority of staff were college students partying.

I wound up traveling for COVID.

I will never forget the screams.

I have the mildest COVID story compared to most nurses but I'm still pissed.

I worked in long term care. I had just gone part time to pursue my Nurse Practitioner degree. We had to get swabbed twice a week. Rapid swabs weren't available early on- we had to get full on PCRs. I had to help with that instead of caring for residents but we were staffed just fine. Every time staff complained/joked about me poking their brain I would tell them there's nothing to poke - I was sick of it. I had to pick my nose too!

We were getting regulations so many times a day. We would have major announcements three times a day sometimes. The Department of Health was spamming emails.

We had angry family members threaten us because we were following DOH rules. We had the county executive and families protesting in our parking lot calling us the worst things as if we had a choice.

I was working during winter break. Finally the vaccine! Our entire facility was COVID free for nine months! Not one resident got sick! We got the first vaccine on December 23rd. All of the residents that consented, and half of the staff. We were forced to take an admission from the local hospital who allegedly didn't have COVID. He had dementia and wandered and HAD to go to memory care. We fought corporate and they told us we were being selfish, and it was our DUTY to empty the hospital. We just wanted to keep our residents safe.

To no one's surprise, he ended up having COVID, discovered after he wandered all over then became symptomatic after. We lost 27 residents in 6 weeks. I wasn't there for most of it. I of course, got COVID- tested positive Jan 1st. We also only had 1 size of N95 which, after being fit tested 2 years later, I discovered was NOT my size. When I was allowed to come back to work after 2 weeks everything was in shambles. Patient 0 was still there. I came back as an overnight supervisor. He died that night. I called his wife in to see him with 10 minutes to spare. It was snowing so hard. He was just made a DNR that day. I was glad, because I didn't want to put a trash bag over someone's head to do CPR like we were instructed to for COVID. I was angry at him. An agency nurse and I swabbed his nose to see if he was still positive from 4 weeks ago and he still was.

My own grandmother was in our facility and I wasn't allowed to visit her. She died the next Christmas. I called family when I heard about the mandate so they could see her one last time before the weird regulations for nursing home visits.

I was the unit manager on the dementia unit when I first started here. I moved to rehab and assistant director of nursing, but I admitted 3/4 of those patients. Half of those knew me from when I was but a little resident care assistant in assisted living. I knew some of these people for almost 10 years. Their families too of course. I have so many little trinkets from them and I know the names of the resident's whose family gave them to me. A little crochet cow, a clay pot, a wine bottle with Christmas lights in it, a picture frame... I sorted through all of the belongings that were piled up in the shower room because me and a few other staff were the only ones that could recognize family photos and resident's clothes. It was just weird. I was so empty inside.

My coworker who must have had an N95 that actually fit told me they had just one CNA per unit. She would feed someone breakfast and they would be just fine… then they would be dead by lunch.

So like, no, I don't respect you if you don't take the vaccine or wear a mask. Not one bit. I extend to you the same care that was extended to my family/residents.

I can't even read anyone else's story because I am not ready to revisit any of this ever.

I worked acute psych throughout the pandemic. Not many patients of mine died, but there were so, so, so, so many people who decompensated either due to getting COVID, or due to not being able to access outpatient care/medications due to (valid) COVID restrictions. Many of our patients who got COVID recovered fully physically, but never attained their pre-COVID level of functioning. In our unit, we were wholly unequipped to handle isolation precautions, taping plastic over patients doors as a "barrier". Not being linked with a medical hospital, or even considered a hospital to most supply providers, we were last on the list to get gowns, masks, or respirators.

I have so many but I just don't want to talk about it anymore. I haven't been all that different but I'm not the same. I've pulled back from my MAGA family members because people like them yelled at us every day for over a year. Said horrible shit. Threatened us, called the cops, screamed at us on the phone, I have so much hatred in my heart for MAGA because of what they did to not just me, but the entire country. Fucking narcissistic selfish assholes, the entire lot of them.

The country betrayed us when they couldn't get haircuts.

I have no obligation to the country anymore.

You put a patient in front of me and I'll treat them as I'd want my most loved ones treated, all day, every day.

No exaggeration: the lady brought in by police for psych clearance after she'd been found to have smothered her 6 yr old son, drug dealers and addicts, the prisoner with Nazi tattoos blaring Fox news, the boomers blaring Fox news... I'll treat them with the same kindness I treat the sweetest and most vulnerable among us. Ok really, I go above and beyond for the vulnerable. But still, I show up to do my job and whoever they put in front of me will get anywhere from my most adequate to my very best.

I don't care how gaslit they are.

And do you know why?

Because I'm not going to change them and I'm sure as fuck not going to let them change me.

Will I correct them when they say shit that's wrong? Yup.

Will I waste effort on them? Nope.

My job is to treat them right and then go home and raise my kids to not turn out like them.

Because my paycheck will not change either way.

The death that broke me was a fully vaccinated 59yr old who had long standing cardiac issues. She was transferred to me at the start of handover, I was told she was palliative and not for escalation. She arrived on a 15L trauma mask, her two sons in tow, stable.

Within two hours, her sats had dropped and she was starting to become agitated and panicky, trying to leap out the bed and tear her facemask off. I went into her file to get the Just In Case prescription for a lovely hit of midazolam which helped with the hypoxia panic... And the doctor hadn't prescribed anything.

I called the overnight team, who said they were slammed, and would get to me soon. By the time they arrived it was after midnight (I'd been working since 7.30pm). The advanced nurse practitioner (ANP) put a further 5L nasal cannula under the trauma mask and began reading the notes. I had to see to another patient (1:12 ratio on nightshift) and when I came out the son said "She had to run off, she said she will be back.

I checked the prescription, still no midazolam. The additional oxygen had helped though. For a whole hour. Then, on 21L of oxygen, her sats began dropping again. 80%. 75%. She began panicking again, sheer terror on her face. She was letting out little gasping screams. The sons were trying to hold her down in the bed (we are not allowed) and I'm trying to reassure her. She is sweating, her blonde hair plastered against the side of her face and sticking up around the mask holding elastic. It's 3am. No sign of a doctor or ANP. I call the overnight number again, and she answers breathlessly. "I'm sorry, I got called to a peri-arrest, and now a cardiac arrest. I'll be with you shortly.

The patient's oxygen sats dropped to 70%. We tried to reposition her. She wouldn't tolerate the proning, so agitated, but we tried anyway. Her bowels exploded and we cleaned her up, watching her colour turn to blue as we quickly changed the sheets beneath her having had to flatten the bed to do so. 4am. I'm staring at the controlled drugs cupboard. Midazolam is a schedule 3 or 4, so not subject to needing two nurses, but it's also still locked up because it's a powerful sedative. If I give that without a prescription for it, I'd be breaking not only hospital policy, but the law and the Nursing and Midwifery code of conduct. Not only could I be struck off, but I could potentially be jailed.

But my patient would be given peace and dignity in her final hours.

I battled with myself, to and fro, and checked the system again just before five am. Finally the script was on.

Midazolam can be administered hourly and she was so agitated by this point it took two doses, along with some morphine to slow her resp rate and alleviate any pain, before she stopped thrashing about like a Tasmanian devil. Sats were sitting around about 70% still, heart rate had come down but still badly in AF. My healthcare assistant and I tidied her up and repositioned her, but this time the oxygen saturations didn't come up. I went to hand over, and then the dayshift nurse and I signed out more midaz and morphine. I popped into the room first, she was sitting at 47%. I told the family that the 21l of oxygen had stopped working, and converted her, with their permission, back to 5l nasal cannula for comfort. "It won't be long," I said. "We'll come back in with some more medicine to keep her comfortable."

By the time the dayshift nurse went in with the medicine, she had passed. I'd not even managed to get out of my uniform and into my civvies yet. And I was *mad* angry. And sad. That woman had suffered. Really suffered. But it wasn't the fault of the admitting doctor, ED had over 40 people waiting to be seen, with capacity for 30 bedspaces, including resuscitation and pediatrics (it's a small hospital). The admissions ward was equally busy and short on nurses. The consultant had to review and ensure speedy transfer of the wall of patients. The most junior doctors had only just started a month before, so were probably in need of a guiding hand, which wasn't there on a Sunday night during Delta season. And the overnight team were short staffed and overwhelmed that night by what proved to be a most fatal night for a lot of people, with one peri arrest, one cardiac arrest, one massive brain bleed following a fall from a very anti-coagulated older male, a major hemorrhage and several other catastrophes including a pregnant woman with COVID de-satting, who had been sent to the only hospital in the area without maternity services and the other hospital was kicking up about taking a COVID positive mother to be. She was 24 weeks along.

And that's when the enormity of it all hit me. The realisation that the system was broken and COVID had taken the remainder of everything that was left and was slowly grinding it all to dust. That day I barely slept and when I could, the patient's face and her breathless little screams would appear before me.

I took a month out and got a psychologist, as well as a review by a psychiatrist. Intensive learning how to build up resilience. Our ward turned back from COVID to Gastro/gen med and I returned, able to focus enough on patient care to be an effective nurse. The HCA who was working with me that night is still off, with diagnosed PTSD (she is a young woman, and took the nearly daily deaths quite badly).

I still see the patient in my head sometimes. It's hard to say to myself that I did everything I could, because I knew I could have violated all the rules and put my career in jeopardy, and saved hours of distress for this woman. But if I had, there was going to be patients afterwards who would have needed me too, and I wouldn't have been there.

I think COVID nursing, and nursing during COVID times, is changing us all. And it is a painful and dark metamorphosis, so I am so glad this forum exists so I can see it's not just me, but that other nurses from all across the globe are experiencing this same horror and heartbreak. It's good to talk.

I will never forget the deaths, so much death. I did Med-Surg/ Telemetry and ICU. I did so much post-mortem care I never want to do it again for the rest of my life.

In ICU, a lot of the patients were CPAP or BIPAP until they decompensated and needed to be intubated, sedated with Propofol & Fentanyl drips, blood pressure managers with Levophed & Epinephrine drips, additional drips, tube feedings, proning patients, third spacing, watching their oxygen sats dropping with no improvement.

I still have PTSD from taking care of COVID patients (like a lot of us do from the pandemic) which is why I decided to go into a totally different field and work as a nurse only when I wanted to. A lot of these hospitals didn't have even enough PPE for the healthcare professionals working in the trenches. I got so disgusted because the hospitals were looking at patients as a number and not a person. I was over it.

I forget how much I don't think about it until I talk with other healthcare professionals in detail about it. I just bummed myself out replying to this post.

I was in ICU, but not for OG COVID, transferred March 2021, so I experienced that brief lull, and then Delta hit. During my orientation, the lull was in full swing in my rural area, and I didn't have a COVID patient the entire 8 weeks. When Delta hit, I had to learn so much on the fly. Here's some of the situations that I think about often:

That BiPAP stage. There is so much anxiety, and I have serious PTSD to this day with certain BiPAP patients. Part of it is knowing that this is the last step before intubation and likely never getting off that vent. I've rushed into countless rooms, PPE be damned, because the patient has ripped off their mask and sats are in the 60s. They all always have that same wild fear in their eyes. They know they are suffocating to death. I would sometimes just pray that I'd come back and the patient would be intubated, because it didn't seem fair to keep up the torture. They could have sedation and pain control, and I hope some semblance of peace.

The lonely deaths. Had quite a few of these. I believe I have a post about the one that hit me the hardest if you check my history. Very closely related to the next topic….

FaceTime with the Family. I always hated doing this, especially as a night shift nurse. I'll never forget one COVID patient in particular. She was vented and had a chest tube that would not stop oozing blood from the site. It was a horror show every time I came in. Well, I come in one night and the nurse hands me a post-it with like 6 telephone numbers on it. I was to make a big, ol' FaceTime group chat for all these family members for this patient…at 2200. And for some reason this was prioritized. Forget the meds, forget my other patients; I'm going to be tied up, in full PPE, HEPA filter in full blast in the background, trying to speak loudly enough through an N95 with a mask on top of it to give this lady's entire family some false hope. I remember having just enough time to cover up any signs of bleeding on her linens, and positioning her head in a way that she appeared comfortable…like she was sleeping. I make it through and everyone hangs up except the daughter. She stays on and brings her young kids into frame. She asks me some questions, I remember trying not to sugarcoat things as I'm hearing her kids ask about their grandma. Is she sleeping? When is she coming home? Damn. Starting to wrap things up, I think I'm in the clear, but hold on, one more thing, why the fuck can't y'all do her hair? Huh? Now I'm Black, and my patient is Black, but I can guarantee she won't want me to do her hair. I can barely do my hair. I'm also the only Black nurse on this unit. But also your momma is trying to die, but if you insist on her looking Casket Sharp, I'll see what I can do. Priorities.

The anti-vax angle. We had nurses quitting after my health system started mandating vaccination. It was so frustrating, because as a profession rooted in science and based on observations, we knew what happened to the unvaccinated. It was also frustrating to hear all of the anti-vax views from patients, switch their TVs to Fox News, and prepare for their imminent intubation. I've had more than one patient express regret for not getting vaccinated when it was way too late.

Hopelessness We all knew how most of these cases would end. In 2021, if you were unvaccinated, in your 60s, and had a co-morbidity, you only had a variable amount of time left and it would be pure torture. We put so much energy into keeping these people alive for one more day, one more hour, one more minute. Success was measured in shifts. Did you make it until 0705? It was a good day. I really think morale suffered and it was a long time before humor found its way back to my unit. I also think so much of that expended, negative energy hung around for a while, and I believe it influenced so much interpersonal negativity afterwards. We lost a lot of staff, and many just weren't the same.

My personal anxiety. It truly suffered and I'm sure many feel the same. If I worked my 3s in a row, it was a guarantee that I wouldn't sleep between shifts. When I could sleep, I was having fevered dreams about working. I was never off. The anxiety I felt before a shift was palpable. I took the stress home. I started drinking more. It's gotten better, but I'm always waiting for that next wave.

I never worked in the ICU, but I did work on a floor for almost a year that was a Medical Surgical unit turned last minute into a full time step down COVID unit. I'd been a nurse for barely a year at that point, but… the amount of deaths, the amount of codes, the amount of wheeling patients into the ICU, watching their heart rate and their oxygen drop, their body changing colors, their hands and feet being ice cold, the ragged and rattling in their final breaths, patients being so scared, so so scared… begging you with their eyes to save them. And you the nurse, fighting so hard to keep someone alive when deep down you know they aren't going to make it, trying not to feel anything because if you do, you might break… your family doesn't get it, at home it's like talking to a wall. Your coworkers are so burnt out sometimes you don't know if talking about it will help or just create more depression/anxiety or maybe have them change the way they look at you.

I do truly believe that in the final moments of death, people know when someone is with them in the room, people know when someone cares. I truly think in moments like those nurses do not understand how important they are.

Personally I left the bedside because I couldn't handle the PTSD, the nightly panic attacks, and dreading waking up in the morning. I do Home Health case management now and I'm happy, which is something I didn't think could happen for me in this job.

Please know you're not alone.

After the vaccine, I was assigned a newly admitted patient. Standard story, long term chronic dialysis patient who got COVID and now was hypoxic and requiring oxygen for the first time in their lives. I was so cynical by this point, I thought, "Here we go again," and prepared myself for that sight of some half-dead looking person in a hospital bed.

Instead I walked in and found the patient up, walking around their room independently, no oxygen needed at all. I was completely floored. The nephrologist later told me that the patient was one of the first in the entire state of Massachusetts who was hospitalized *after* having received the COVID vaccine. We knew this because the state was tracking those numbers so closely. The night and day difference in outcomes before and after the vaccine was unbelievable.

All of a sudden, we stopped losing all of our patients. Still lots of death happening, no doubt, but it was more the people who were already so sick before they got COVID that you weren't surprised when they died. But the younger, healthier ones stopped showing up in the hospital, and when they did, they recovered fast and went home. It felt like the sun came out from behind clouds after a long storm.

Paramedic who worked in the ER during COVID- we had a hospital we shipped our patients to because it was bigger and more equipped. Until they had no room. Then we kept them in our ICU. Most of the ER and hospital wouldn't set foot in the COVID corner. Almost all the ER nurses got notes from their doctors about how they couldn't work in the Covid area because of (whatever). So I was there along with a few specific nurses every day. I also transported all COVID patients to the ICU. They kept a tally of how many of them went home. For weeks, the tally never moved. I'd bring patients in, a few every day, and the number never moved. I asked them if they counted the ones shipped to the other hospital, thinking 'well, maybe they didn't die, they just were transferred, not D/Ced home'. Nope. No one got transferred.

I held people's hands while they were being prepped for intubation. I had to let very sick people go home because we needed the room for the dying. The MDs and PAs spoke to patients over a phone. Sometimes I was the only person they'd see the whole time in the ER.

The tension got so bad the nurses would have screaming fights about whose turn it was to go into the COVID Corner. Not because they were bad nurses, but because they were so exhausted and traumatized.

I didnt work in COVID ICU or even purposefully the COVID units.

I worked in periop. Pre op/pacu for the main OR. Because the rest of the hospital was burning down with COVID patients there were NO ROOMs for regular surgical patients. We did cancel a lot of electives for a while. Maybe a couple weeks until they decided that wasn't feasible anymore and they really needed the income. But some of those patients really really needed their surgeries (cancer patients for example). This started off a new trend of "everybody is now going home outpatient". When we asked what would happen if somebody couldn't go home because God forbid something bad happens, what do we do? Admin responded with essentially "that won't ever happen tho silly lol"

Queue us resuming all surgeries. Keep in mind we were a smaller hospital and our OR actually closed overnight except emergencies (our emergencies being the odd lap appy or testicular torsion, we are not any form of heart hospital or stroke center, very few people actually took call).

I sent home during this period:

-a below the elbow arm amputation, outpatient. Wtf

-a hip replacement that needed 2 units of blood intraop and when I asked in recovery if I should check an h/h prior to discharge I was told no and to send them home. They went out the door hypotensive, nauseous and pale on the hospitals and doctors insistance. Like..what am I supposed to do? I told them to return to the ER if there's anything that feels sus.

-a Michael J Fox style Parkinsons patient who had an elective joint replacement. Fell, trying to get out of the car at home and broke the affected leg.

-we tried to send home various XLIFS, TLIFS and open hysterectomies we couldn't get the pain under control of to get them off the stretcher and out the door.

-TURPS that bled all over the place and the elderly wife or ride home would stare at us in bewilderment when we tried to explain how they needed to flush the catheter frequently to prevent clots because we couldn't send them home on a bladder irrigation.

-multilevel ACDFs who popped a hematoma and had to come back for emergent evacuation and end up on a vent.

-had people have anaphylactic reactions to ancef suddenly, hernia repairs who coded suddenly, surgeries we just couldn't get to wake up or their vital signs under control or who had heart attacks in recovery.

Nowhere for these patients to go but either home or we had to draw straws to stay the night with these patients. Again, most of the periop nurses in particular were no night, no call, no weekends and now suddenly everybody was forced to stay 16-24hour shifts, weekend shifts or overnight shifts to hang out with patients who would normally need to be admitted.

Our hospital became so overran with COVID patients that our icu which used to be such a low level icu that they housed bilateral knee replacements, now had to learn how to be icu nurses. Even us in periop, we're given 2 icu online modules to complete so we could turn pacu into a COVID icu overflow. Had no training with any experienced icu nurse. Just given the 2 online modules.

It was a crapshoot. I stayed over one night for one of our regular cancer patients who'd usually stay the night. He was fine. I didn't mind watching him. They begged me to come back the next night for the same thing. I came in and he was discharged and instead had 3 ventilated icu patients on drips and I was by myself. I asked what I was supposed to do if I needed help and was told to just call the house supervisor. I was so pissed.

But anyway. The entire thing was a bizarre fever dream. We had family members threaten us with physical violence for sending patients home or how they thought they'd have a room available and then didn't. I saw notes in charts that said things like "cancelled due to no room in hospital". We went from testing everybody for COVID before they got to the hospital to testing only some people and giving them grace and testing them in pre op for them to come back positive and expose everybody in the department and waiting room. Got physical threats for performing the COVID test.

Specifically though I remember crying because I was alone (husband was on deployment and stuck because of COVID lockdown) and I was just so hungry. I hadn't worked nights in years and was forced to work nights because of COVID and I got off work and went to the grocery store and everybody panic bought everything. All that was left at the grocery store was off brand cocopuffs and I lived off that for a few days. I legit teared up in the store holding this lone bag of cocopuffs. Lmao. Atleast I was rich in toilet paper.

Before I went into nursing I worked at a funeral service during COVID. Actually COVID is what made me want to become a nurse. We had to get 2 cooler trailers for all the bodies to keep up while our 2 walkins were full. We ran the crematory 24 hours a day the entire time of thw outbreak. All the other funeral homes were full trying to find places to put all the decedents. We constantly were picking up COVID cases in our large metro area in nursing homes, icus, and the corner's offices. It was horrible! There are few things I wish people knew 1 the amount of elderly people who commuted suicide during this time out of fear and loneliness. 2. The corners had to mark some deaths as COVID when they really werent the cause of death due to policy at the time such as when they had it a month before and died in a motorcycle accidents etc. 3. We lost a lot of good people who we worked with dying from exposure from decedent with COVID. It was a bad time in the world I wish to never see again.

New grad MedSurg nurse during that time

The thing that stuck out to me was how quickly people declined. Our ICU were overflowing so we kept some on MedSurg. Families unable to say goodbye to their loved ones that they'd have to come up to the window to see them. Had one guy who came in who was on 2L NC that in the course of my shift went up to 6L. Came back the next night and he was maxed out on airvo.

It was also insane how people and hospital admin treated us. Doctors were using my assessment notes to say they saw the patient, when in reality, they watched them from the doorway, never stepping in. Housekeeping wouldn't empty any trash or give linens or anything, so we had to do everything. We were so short and no admin ever came to help. It really spoke volumes of how dispensable nurses were. I never had anyone code but I had so many people who should have but did during the day

The other thing was we had so many ltc patients because all acute facilities were backed up. So we were running without aides and having 3-5 total cares in our patient load and barely having enough nurses to be able to take care of them. Psych patients lingered on our unit for weeks and weeks and we just were not equipped. High acuity patients being dropped off but no 1:1 sitter so you're trying to sit on them while watching 4 other patients.

For me it wasn't necessarily the sick people. But the mental toll of having critically sick and knowing no one was coming to help.

The closest I've ever come to wartime medicine. They even used words like "deployed" when talking about the outpatient providers who were asked to work inpatient bc there wasn't enough help. I am pretty sure I have ptsd from it.

I'm the spouse of an ER nurse in the Bay Area. I still remember with dread the day she texted me from work "we ran out of the good masks." At the peak in 2020 I was worried every day that I was sending her to her death, or God forbid, sending her to bring death home to our kid.

I am an OT. I worked in a rural SNF during COVID. The area I work was and still is extremely resistant to vaccines, which exacerbated the problem substantially. Thankfully our facilities ownership took it seriously and locked its down fast. We were able to survive until late Septemeber 2020 with only minimal deaths. Then it got in somehow despite the heavy lock down, the lack of family visits, the mandated weekly testing of all residents and staff. Literally half of the staff came down with it within the same week. Nursing, rehab, dietary, environmental, everyone got hit. And then the residents caught it. 11 deaths in one week. Then they just kept getting sick and dying. Families were unable to say goodbye to their dying loved ones in person. They had to say their last goodbyes through a freaking window. It was awful. So many died and so many were sick in our community we had to turn and entire wing into a COVID wing. And of course there were the supply shortages so we where having to try to reuse the masks, faceshields, gowns (not between workers, just saving your own items and reusing them). It was terrible.

Do you remember that in the beginning, we had no way to even test for COVID? Back in the spring of 2020 when NYC was the epicenter of the virus, everyone working in the greater metro area (NY, NJ, CT) had a hospital of patients and no real way to tell who was actually positive. The only way to get a test was to be symptomatic, be hospitalized, and then the test took two days to come back. We got good at looking at other labs like the CRP (since C-19 is an inflammatory virus) to make educated guesses.

And not enough PPE. Only the staff in the C-19 floors had N-95s, so the staff on the "clean" floors kept getting sick. RNs on cardiac telemetry were getting one single mask (not n-95, just regular paper mask) per week. And because the ICU was all C-19, the STEMIs fresh from the cath lab were going to the regular tele floor.

When I worked on C-19 floors, I'd get an n-95 each shift, but one of their quirks was the polyurethane straps would expend, but we're not elastic to expand and retract, so once it was on and fitted, I couldn't remove it and get another seal if I put it back on. So I would do my whole shift without eating or drinking anything. While sweating because I was wearing plastic isolation gowns, and moving patients in my own because we were limiting how many people went into rooms. And then we had a gown shortage, too, just one per shift, so I would gear up, and spend the whole shift behind the "dirty line" on the floor and would ask "clean" staff to get me the supplies and medications I needed.

That does not even go into the deaths. So many deaths. Every shift someone would pass or transition to CMO. And the ones who survived, but were not well. Like my otherwise healthy 50-year-old who survived intubation, but ended up on dialysis after clots screwed up his kidneys.

I have seen a lot of death in a trauma ICU, but your team could always get around a big save and some patients with horrible traumas could make it through their hospitalization and still live a life meaningful to them. I think the part that hurt the most was we could do everything for patients with COVID ARDS and they just didn't get better. I think it was most defeating around thanksgiving and I was as a fellow getting calls via the transfer center asking to discuss transfer for ECMO on people around my age or younger and declining 'until we had or bed or circuit available' knowing that you were the 4th or 5th hospital called and that none of your patients were coming off pump anytime soon. Short runs were 2-3 weeks, but often longer. Preparing families for what was essentially an eternity, and knowing they couldn't be there unless they died was breaking.

My husband, an MD (IM and ID) who was vaccinated for Covid, was very unlucky and almost died from Covid. He was in a university hospital ICU on a vent, then vent with trach, pressors, dialysis, proned-the whole 9 yards. Wanted me to make him a no code. Got a hospital acquired multi drug resistant infection. Was on the biggest gun antibiotics that exist. Went to LTC. Didn't get such great care. He was oversedated. Every time he had a problem/side effect of current drugs, their answer would be to add another drug. They didn't know the drugs they gave him caused urinary retention. They didn't know the multiple sedatives he was getting were causing him psychosis. (I know there is ICU psychosis and sundowning but as soon as he was weaned from the sedatives his mentation was fine). It was a nightmare. Finally got off the vent and the trach. Then to another rehab to learn to walk again and do ADLs. Then he was home and got PT, OT, and a once a week nurse visit. I, a peds RN by trade, changed his sacral decubitus ulcer dressing twice a day. I researched and purchased the latest in wound care supplies. I made protein smoothies and steaks and fresh squeezed OJ and gave him B 12 shots (his primary care recommended to try to help with foot drop nerve damage). I ordered shoes for his AFOs. We were hemorrhaging money because of the poor type of disability insurance he had. Kid in college trying to keep going. Kid in Jr High trying to keep going. It was ALL TOO REAL. He is good now. Still has some footdrop. Has diminished exercise capacity. But you wouldn't know it to interact with him. No preexisting conditions. Mid 50s. Shout out to all the University ER and ICU doctors, nurses, RTs, housekeepers and lab folks.

I worked in the ER as a nurse during all of Covid. Half of our ER was full of vented Covid patients, most of whom ended up dying. We had no visitors allowed so we were the ones forced to uphold the rules and turn families away while their loved ones died alone. I coded numerous previously healthy patients, some my own age of 30, knowing that even if I got ROSC they would end up dying anyways. Codes were run through the glass with only one doctor, one nurse, and one RT in the room. We had no PPE. We had to use the same N95 for months as someone had "stolen" our PPE supply. I was convinced the entire time I was working that I would inevitably die from COVID. Just of matter of when, not if. I had to deal with the naysayers gaslighting me and telling me that COVID wasn't real while I was living every day through the worst parts of it. I had to deal with the loneliness of being a pariah due to how exposed I was. Friends and family no longer allowed me in their houses. I ate meals outside or in the garage alone. I stripped and showered as soon as I got home from work every day, afraid to spread Covid to my family and kill them.

I remember the day we all were Covid vaccinated the first time. We were in a conference room at the hospital spread 6 feet apart. Silent tears of thankfulness running down many of my colleagues faces as we realized that we may finally have some protection from death.

The PTSD we suffer as healthcare workers from this time has gone unacknowledged by the world. No emotional or psychological support was ever offered. It's impossible to talk to anyone who didn't experience working in a hospital during the pandemic because many people seem to forget or feign ignorance that it ever occurred

I worked at the bedside in the ER through the whole pandemic and one thing I haven't heard almost anyone talk about is how the pediatricians and primary care folks went wholly and completely above and beyond to keep folks out of our waiting room during the worst of things. One peds outfit I know staffed her clinic open seven days a week, and on call, while our hospital and pediatric unit was running at a maybe 150% capacity, with new grads running PICU beds. Even the urgent care folks, who we joke could be replaced by a monkey that has a button which randomly assigns "z-pack" or "go to the ER", they did everything they could. I don't know how bad it would have gotten if they hadn't been there. I don't really want to know. I do know we wouldn't have made it.

I'm a hospital SW and covered the Covid ICU during the pandemic. Work on a team of 10 and will never forgive my supervisor for sending them all to work from home but leaving 3 of us (myself, the trauma SW and psych SW alone in the hospital). Our teammates were supposed to do what they could via phone with the understanding they'd come in person at least a few times per week to manage face-to-face needs. This didn't happen and instead they'd call us and dump extra work in our laps while we were already drowning.

I experienced the "public" (families, patients) as aggressive, angry, screaming, accusatory and outright hostile. People screaming at us that Covid wasn't real while their person lay dying from it, saying we were fabricating the diagnosis for government kickbacks, sitting in care conferences with families demanding hydroxychloroquine "or else", people literally spitting in my face, watching my entire unit die in a single day, then the beds fill back up and start again.

Hosting deaths over zoom while families trash talked us in the background. A woman who drove her cancer patient friend in for a planned admission (5+ hour road trip) found out they were Covid positive, then she turned around and went back to her job doing in home caregiving for the elderly because 'Covid isn't any worse than the flu'.

Or, the one I'll never forget. The patient so sick they were maxed out on hiflo O2 (the kind that comes from the wall) and couldn't stand, barely hanging on. Family insisting again- COVID isn't real and they're taking their person home. Patient wants to leave. We pleaded with them for hours, trying to help them understand that their person would not survive long enough to get to the car in the parking lot if we unhooked them from the oxygen. I remember a conversation in the hallway with my charge and fellow asking if there were medications or what could we do to make it less traumatic for the family-because we knew the patient was going to go into respiratory distress and likely die in the elevator as soon as they left.

I was stretched to my limit with families blaming me for the visitation restrictions, lonely patients dying without loved ones present and also fearing for my spouse's wellbeing who is an RN and had been recalled back to work in ICU alongside me without proper PPE.

Covid broke whatever faith I had left in humanity. People were ugly, cruel, hostile and aggressive to all of the staff. They were careless- spreading illness and then expecting (demanding) compassion when they showed back up sick and dying. Screaming and blaming. It was awful.

I'm still in the same job though my entire team except for one other person quit, most of my ICU staff have left- and I'm struggling to figure out how to move forward and have compassion again after seeing nothing but the darkest sides to humanity for those years. The public has changed overall and I'm left feeling scarred and damaged.

DMV/NJ/PA ERs: Got rocked. Smoked out. I volunteered like a dumbass bc I felt that my older colleagues were at greater risk, since I am very athletic and my immune system is pretty rock solid. I had no clue what I was walking into. PAPRs and bunny suits in some places, if the facilities had money, until supplies began running out, then it became BYOG—being your own gear or get stuck using trash bags and recycled months-old N95s. Code Blue alerts going off hourly, often times with just 2 RNs at a time, families threatening to storm the hospital because of the no-visitor policy, battling acne from wearing sweaty, gross masks, cloth gowns, and tape and goggles. Colleagues who refused COVID assignments would yell at you for being too close to them in the cafeteria lines. People dropping like flies in the WR, or sometimes just found stiff when their names were finally called—they weren't asleep, they had been dead for some time. Stretchers flying across main lobbies with teams performing CPR and attempting to break world records in stretcher racing. So many goddamn alarms going off. Colleagues crying, swearing, losing their ever loving minds. Some codes were short, less than half an hour, other codes were 3-4 hours long, blood, piss, urine on used supplies thrown onto the floor because the trash cans had long since been overfilled. Yeah, I did not know. I fucked up.

Almost lost a 12-year old from peritonitis because he had to sit in my waiting room for nine hours waiting to be seen. And he was a priority patient. He was seen before lots of other folks. It was only because our charge nurse left our unit secretary in charge and went to personally do his lab work- and I'm pretty sure she ordered his ultrasound without telling the doc who was up to their eyeballs in shit, but I don't know that for sure and I don't want to know, because that would be practicing medicine and hugely illegal. But otherwise the kid might have set out there longer. Which would have been catastrophic because his appendix had burst like a fucking balloon. We tried to transfer him to a nearby Level One Trauma Center that had a full pediatric surgery service, but they said no. They refused! They refused a kid who needed emergency surgery or else they'd die because they were holding pediatric patients in the hallway of their ER. We finally had to fly them to another state, another state, to get them to somewhere that would accept them. And then I had to go home and be told by my father in law that it was all a hoax, that I didn't know what I'd actually seen.

Microbiology lab tech checking in. We are a regional hub lab that does all of the testing for all of our sites in our area (large well known hospital system in our area). There were 10 of us at the time able to do all of the COVID testing. 10 of us setting up 2500+ tests a day on top of all of our normal work ups. We were the only people able to test and, at the time the tests were 4+ hours to run. People were calling non-stop for critical results because patients were dying, patients needed surgery or transfers that weren't able to go without a COVID result. One time I had a nurse pleading with me to run a patient faster because they were tanking fast and the sound of defeat when they were told it would be at least 3 more hours was grim. Doctors were putting in orders for their own swabs as stats constantly and we would get absolute profanity rained upon us for not letting them go before critical patients. The tests were not super accurate at first and sometimes repeats would not be the same, so the lab was blamed for doing something clearly. Supplies were so short we ran out of gloves rated for chemo drugs and had to use gloves akin to lunch lady gloves and hope nothing would leach through. Our biosafety hood actually broke and we didn't notice until the testing agency came in and told us. We were so busy running around we didn't hear the fan dying. No idea how long it took before it was found we were running COVID and tb specimens without aerosol protection. We were reusing masks for up to a week, putting them into paper bags between uses. We had constant supply issues that sometimes we would be out of reagents for other tests for up to a month despite attempts to acquire it. Sometimes we had 40 hours of overtime on a pay-period. There were times people went more than a month without a day off. There were blocks on PTO so even though we accrued it we could not use it. We couldn't hire more help because of a hiring freeze, not that we would have had time to train them anyways. Our morgue was over run and we had to get refrigerator trucks brought in for the overflow. There were several times we would call upstairs with a critical positive csf or blood culture only to have nobody available to answer right away because of short staffing. We lost so many great techs due to burn out, many choosing to leave healthcare entirely.

ER social worker here. I remember a wife sitting in her car outside the emergency room while we worked desperately to save her husband. She was alone as all their kids were out of state. I put a blue heart in his window (his favorite color) so she knew which room was his.

I went to her car outside. We had intubated and proned him, and were waiting for an ICU bed to open. We were holding sometimes for days in our ER, and really the only way ICU beds were opening was when someone died. She was alone in her car sobbing and said "he could die from this?" And I said yes, he could. We are doing our best. She said "what if I never see him again".

I broke the rules and snuck her in the side door, which was only two rooms away from her husband. She wore a paper mask with an N95 over it. I told someone "she is a patient looking for the bathroom" and we walked to her husband's room. She could see him through the window on the door, but he was already in the pronating bed and was upside down- she could see his legs 😭 😭 😭 I'll never forget her hand on that window and then having to walk her away.

ER and ambulance urban area in Georgia. Only bright spot was the short time when they banned all visitors so all we had to deal with was the 200 percent over capacity we were at.

I was working as a hospitalist PA in the Mid-Atlantic region for a large academic hospital. My job was night shift. We ran out of room in the ICU so those patients ended up in the PCU. The PCU patients ended up on my floor which was just a regular med/surg floor. We didn't have enough monitors for these patients so we had to improvise by putting baby monitors in their rooms with the receivers in the nurses station. We literally just had to listen to tell if they were breathing. People who should have been intubated never were because they weren't on the right floor. They were put on CPAP and we hoped for the best. When they were 2 steps from death, we would play games with beds and shift someone out of the ICU down to the PCU and then someone from the PCU to the floor. People died as a result. Totally inappropriate admissions but it was what happened back then.

About 4 weeks into the first wave, I developed COVID from lack of proper PPE (just given an N95, no hood or PAPR). I was sick for 3 weeks and was left with debilitating migraines that I still have today. So far, I've been admitted twice for intractable migraines and I'm not sure it won't happen again. Every day is a guessing game of whether or not I'll be in pain.

I remember when we weren't allowed to wear even our homemade masks on the floors because "It might make the patients nervous." I remember being given isolation gowns that literally fell apart as you took them out of the packaging. I remember being given gowns that if you squirted a flush at them it went right through. I remember finally switching to reusable cloth gowns and that being 1000x better.

I remember reprocessed N95s where the elastic snapped when you tried to put them on. I remember being the last person a lot of people saw because we didn't have enough iPads for FaceTime. I remember having to tell a brand new nurse (graduated a year after me) to push the fucking morphine on their hospice patient already because then at least they wouldn't feel like they were suffocating to death.

I remember having one PAPR hood for 2 years. I remember our ER boarding patients for weeks.

Female age 86 who we will name Claire. Early in the pandemic Claire had the two misfortunes. The first was that she got COVID. The second was that she had debility from it but survived. That may not sound horrendous at first glance but it played out dark. She had her cognition intact. She was able to be discharged but due to her functional decline she needed nursing home care. Because she had survived COVID the nursing home clearly knew she had been exposed and had an immune response offering her some protection prior to vaccines being available. As nursing homes saw more and more COVID cases they would move the newly diagnosed to Claire's room because she had already had it.

The new roommate would die mere feet away from her.

She had 9 different roommates in the course of 4 months.

Death after death after death after death after death after death after death after death after death. No family support our counseling as visits were barred during the delta wave. Her spirits cratered.

The ninth death was her. The vibrant family that knew her was notified. Her body taken to the morgue. This grieving family made remote arrangement to honor her life. Her body was taken to the funeral home the family knew and worked with across generations.

The funeral home director got her body and stopped: This is not Claire.

With the ninth death in one room the exhausted nursing home got it wrong and thought it was Claire. It really was just a roommate. Just a roommate, like that death would be any less significant. That family was notified.

I saw Claire a year after her COVID experience as a palliative care consult for failure to thrive. Her family told me this story. Traumatized, bewildered as to what happened, separated from family connections, depleted and now frail. She did not die of COVID, but its heavy hand played a role.

ICU MD checking in.

I work in a relatively small unit. We are usually staffed for somewhere around 15-20 beds. Physical unit has 26 beds. I'm the director of the surgical ICU.

During the delta wave of COVID, we had 26 intubated COVID patients at all times. This was at a high complexity VA; we were one of the only places in the state with any beds at all so any sick COVID veteran within the state (and even a few civilians) got transferred to us.

We had every intensivist and every nurse and RT working every shift around the clock. Anesthesiologists and CRNAs had little surgical work to cover so they served as the airway/lines "hot team." OR RNs were the proning team. MICU docs covered day shift and SICU (me) covered nights. We had leadership surge planning crisis meetings frequently about scarce resource allocation for things like CRRT machines and ventilators. We had no beds for transplant patients. The morgue frequently ran out of space so the overflow bodies went into refrigerated trucks.

Every single one of those patients was unvaccinated. Every single one of those patients died. Some days we had deaths just one after another. As soon as one died, we got another in. We tried to hold off on intubation as long as possible but it was inevitable. I heard and saw so many final conversations between families take place over FaceTime. More than one veteran begged me not to let them die with what would turn out to be their final words. We all knew they would die.

Every time a veteran dies in our ICU, the volunteers and transport staff (most of whom are veterans too, along with tons of our other staff) do a processional where we play a recording of taps and everyone stands silently to honor that veteran as their body is wheeled out of the unit. The veterans on staff stand at attention and salute. It makes me cry every time. We did SO MANY taps processions in those days.

Worked in a clinic as a non-clinical staff member in Appalachia:

I remember a young, healthy patient who finally weaned off oxygen two years after getting COVID. He worked so, so hard in his rehab and even then it took literal years for him to even go about low-intensity tasks without the O2. He also had permanent heart damage.

The shear number of people coughing on us, mask under their chin (we required pts to wear them if they had cough/ cold/ symptoms) while swearing up and down they couldn't have COVID. To no surprise, they had COVID. Some were immediately panicked and rang nonstop so they could get paxlovid.

Others went about their daily routines, no mask, etc. because they didn't believe in COVID/ felt herd immunity was the way to go.

Another patient had been at a neighbor's family reunion. They held it annually, with four generations and dozens of family members present. Unfortunately, an asymptomatic relative who'd TESTED POSITIVE gave great-grandma and great-grandpa COVID. They both died, as did a number of the other elderly relatives. It tore the entire family apart.

I remember hearing about the first Covid patient in the state. And then in our city. And then my hospital. Every other day, it seemed like the rules changed. One day you needed to wear a bunny suit, n95, full face shield, and have a HEPA filter in the room. Then it would change a couple of days later. My hospital put up a mural to honor the nurses. They put up a huge poster with their photos on it. I worked in interventional X-ray. I helped put dialysis catheters in the Covid patients because their kidneys were failing. One day I hugged a CT tech who I had known for maybe 15 years. A few weeks later he was on my table in IR and I was helping out a line in him. I was talking to him wishing for him to get better. He died a couple of months later. Our environmental service guy was an older gentleman who told me he was very scared to go not the room where we did our patients. I would go back in there and get the trash for him and mop the floor. He was worried he would get in trouble. I told him to always come find me if he needed someone to help him. He made it through the pandemic and retired in 2021. We took a photo together on his last night with us. There were coworkers who started working in my department after the mask mandates started. I never knew what they looked like without a mask. It was strange the first time I saw someone I had worked with for a year without a mask and didn't recognize them. I have never been a touchy person. I don't hug people. The CT guy was the only coworker I let hug me. After Covid, I really just wanted to hug people. I feel like a lot of healthcare workers have PTSD from working through this time. It gives me anxiety to think about going into lockdown again. And I hate walking by that damn mural. It's like they didn't think about all the other people who were affected by it.

I'm a doc in a hospital-affiliated urgent care. My job is to keep people out of the ED. I'm good at it and I don't write a lot of antibiotics.

We saw Covid patients all through the pandemic. We saw people before Covid was known to be a thing—we called it "flu C". When Covid was finally recognized, every primary care office around us shut down and sent us their sick patients. If you had a sniffle, you were sent to us. Some of those offices *still* do that.

We had the same PPE you did…reused masks, garbage bags, and cheap-ass gloves that broke just putting them on. In fact, when Covid was first recognized, we were told *not* to mask up because it would "scare the patients". I actually took pictures throughout Covid of our various PPE outfits. Like the ED, we never saw a PAPR/CAPR.

We didn't have to do the end-of-life care, and for that, I'm extremely grateful. But we *did* have to deal with the long lines of very sick people, the anti-maskers who yelled at us for enforcing masking rules (who then passive-aggressively wore the masks wrong on purpose), the ones who yelled that they couldn't possibly have Covid because their symptoms were just those of a sinus infection (sinus pain was one of the most common symptoms), the ones who yelled that they just needed an antibiotic, the ones who yelled that we couldn't prescribe their pain meds that their PCP usually wrote (you know, the PCPs that got a paid vacation while we took a pay cut so our hospital could stay open), the ones who yelled that Covid wasn't real (got that even from first responders), the ones with sats in the 70s-low 80s and CXRs with ground-glass opacities who yelled that they weren't going to the hospital because hospitals were killing people…yeah. It happened. It all happened.

And even some of my family members, who knew I came home and stripped and showered and sanitized every night, afraid of passing Covid to my young child, afraid of dying myself because my husband is already dead and I didn't want to leave our son an orphan…some of those family members don't believe it was as bad as it was.

People these days still roll their eyes at me if I ask if they did a home Covid test. "I didn't know that was still a thing!" they say.

They roll their eyes at me if I ask if they've had a Covid vaccine. They don't know that I cried when I finally got the shot…because I actually contracted Covid *the week before* I was scheduled to get the vaccine when it first came out, and I was convinced I was going to die.

They still talk of the "plandemic" and "scamdemic" in front of me, as if I haven't been diagnosing and treating it for the last 5 years. That death numbers were greatly exaggerated. That even the diagnostic nasal swabs were impregnated with Covid so the numbers could be inflated.

I don't know what I'll do if bird flu takes hold in humans. I don't know if I can do this again.

I was working in Long-term Care as an RN, at the start of the epidemic, and went into the hospital in mid-2021. Most of the patients I work with are elderly or have some kind of health condition that makes them more susceptible to illnesses.

None of the residents (patients) I worked with at the LTC died of COVID precisely because of the vaccine that came out. If the already ill and infirm could survive a COVID vaccination, catch it, then basically come through it as though it was a mild/moderate flu, then that claim that the vaccine was more deadly has no legs to stand on for me. And these were people who **definitely** tested positive.

Rn, southeast ER and ICU. Started the pandemic in the Emergency department, we had fights about who was in triage because some charge nurses thought it should only be people without kids due to the risk. It was empty and just scary at first, then we started getting actual COVID patients and they quickly filled up the designated Covid rooms and we began to see people get sick and die in hours in the ER. Then they told us we didn't have enough ppe and that we were gonna have to make do. Meanwhile admin that showed walked around with clean masks everyday and kept the stock LOCKED in an office. We continued to stack bodies, some of us got sick, things started breaking but the hospital was losing money, security stopped being there overnight and we started getting updates about homeless patients holed up in empty beds. Then they started dropping our pay and benefits! I was making 25$ an hour to watch people die alone in hallways beds and brawl with psych patients and they took away my 401k match and called me a hero with chalk on the sidewalk on the way into and out of a hospital without a single person not wearing scrubs. I ended up working in a Covid ICU by the end of the pandemic, tripled daily, everyone vented crrt proned was everyone everyday, sometimes Ecmo is thrown in sometimes not, but daily multiple codes multiple deaths and we couldn't even get someone to clean the floors for us. Now nobody cares.

Couple years ago my uncle tried to gaslight me a bit.

I responded quietly and forcefully "I saw the fucking bodies. Our morgue was full. We had to rent refrigerator trucks as temp morgues and THEY were full, no it's not the flu, wear your fucking mask, you are exactly the kind of person who'd die from it."

I had a patient having a massive STEMI, a heart attack, with stereotypic EKG changes that make your heartbeat look like tombstones. We went to swab her for COVID and she grabbed my nurse's hand. "Oh, you're THAT kind of hospital. You're one of the ones killing people," she said. She refused any care. We told her it was just to check so the cardiac catheterization lab folks knew if they needed to be in full COVID gear or not, and she didn't believe us. She started pulling leads off of her body, tried to rip her IV out. I eventually almost got down on my knees and begged her to stay, said we wouldn't swab her, just please, let us save her life. I would have absolutely dropped to my knees if it would've made the difference.

She walked out the front door.

She was fully cogent. Seemed reasonably and normally intelligent. But just lost it when we went to swab her nose.

I have no idea what happened to her. I can pray that maybe she made it to another facility. I really hope she did.

I'm not sure if you realize the lengths these people will go through in their delusions about COVID-19.

I literally had someone refuse my care and die 6 hours later because they were told by the news cycle they consumed that steroids and paxlovid were a way to exterminate them, and that we were just putting people on ventilators for their organs.

Early on in the pandemic I had just gotten off of the ambulance and stopped at a gas station to get coffee on the way home. I lived in a moderate sized city in TN. An older gentleman, probably in his 60s, stopped me at the coffee station and asked me if it was real. "Excuse me? I'm not understanding your question."

He proceeded to tell me the news he watched was telling him it was all a lie in order to crack down on the citizenry by the "deep state", and asked me if it was true because "I would know".

I had to just stare at this man a moment, and informed him I had intubated more people in that 3 months than I had in the last 5 years, and that people were dying from this.

Judging from his expression and the way he walked away quickly after that, I'm hoping that dose of reality hit him. But there is a large amount of America that consumes a news ecosystem that tells them explicitly not to believe the hype, and it's all a conspiracy. And will happily sell them fish tank cleaner for 19.99.

I spent a month in New York with FEMA during the height of it.

I was still pretty new to EMS at the time, and my small town hadn't really been hit that hard yet so I had no idea just how bad it was. It started to dawn on me when on our way into the city we had people honking at us and crying and waving and yelling thank you.

The entire city was essentially a mass casualty event in that patients greatly outnumbered available resources. Initially we were tasked with doing IFTs, but before we could even finish checking in they told us we were being reassigned to running 911. FDNY had so many people out sick they couldn't keep up with the call volume, which rivaled that of 9/11.

Literally within seconds of going in service we were dispatched and we ran non-stop for our entire day... and the next day and the next for two weeks straight. It was absolutely relentless. I'd never seen hospitals so overwhelmed. People were getting tubed and vented in the ambulance bay as they deteriorated while waiting for a bed to open up. I saw a nurse collapse from exhaustion mid-report. You'd see refrigerated semi trailers full of bodies getting hauled away as you're dropping off a patient, then you'd come back a few hours later and the new trailer is already full.

I worked on the box leading up to the pandemic. I came down with something, that I got from transporting a patient, in December of 2019 that made me feel like I was drowning on land. I remember being told to show up to work anyways because we were so short staffed, regardless of how many patients I may have infected in the process. Holding the wall times eventually reached nearly 12 hours long, at which point I just said "fuck this, I'm not helping anyone standing here" and accepted a volunteer position for a government COVID response team. We worked 120 hours a week, 7 days a week. They sent us to nursing homes that had collapsed from COVID. And by collapsed, I mean the CNAs and LVNs had straight up abandoned their patients. We'd arrive, this measly team of 2 RNs, 2 medics, 2 EMTs, and find the patients dead or rotting in their beds. Our medical director had essentially given us a blank check in terms of our scope of practice, and many things were done by all care levels that would now be considered absolutely insane. There was a "do what you must" attitude regarding our scope. There often were no relief teams coming to back us up. We oftentimes worked 3 days straight in full PPE. Occasionally, we could take small catnaps curled up on the floor of the SNF in full PPE out of the way of our coworkers. The SNFs never trusted us, yet they were the ones who called us for help. They were afraid we'd fire their personnel or shut them down, in some cases we did. So we'd experience things like SNFs locking us out of certain wings so we couldn't see the conditions/status of patients. We would experience open hostility, stonewalling, and even assault by SNF healthcare workers. We'd end up going outside and peering through the windows, and counting how many dead were lying in beds in the locked wings. The CNAs/LVNs would sometimes be providing ADLs/care to dead patients to try and gaslight us into thinking they were alive, before they could subtly ferry the body out the back to the coroner all in an attempt to skew our data numbers. Some nursing homes/hospice homes were so badly hit that we ran out of room in the dining area to stack bodies, so we started dragging the body bags out into the parking lot. One nursing home we went to, their medical director decided that if one pt in a room of 6 had COVID that they ALL must have COVID. I witnessed many patients die due to this deliberate non-sensical exposure. Many patients, who were receiving max O2 and on the verge of being vented, would beg and plead us for the vaccine. I felt bad at first, but as time went on (and the psychological trauma and burn out kept building), I eventually felt nothing for them. They made their funeral bed and they were going to sleep in it. Some of the patients were in blatant denial, insisting COVID wasn't a real thing; up until I watched them take their last breath. My cousin, a pharmacist at KP, received the first vaccine a month or so before I did. They were not in a patient-facing role. I was working directly with COVID patients on behalf of the government, so I was definitely a bit bitter to see how the vaccine distribution was allocated. I left EMS as the pandemic started to wind down, as did all my coworkers. The other former teams and personnel I still talk to, I'd say maybe 20% still work in healthcare. The burnout and trauma made some of them reclusive. I and many of my coworkers developed substance abuse disorders and severe PTSD from the experience. An informal survey going around my hospital in the ICUs and ED asked the physicians/RNs and other staff if they would work through another pandemic. A resounding ~80% said they would quit. Do with that what you will. To avoid doxxing myself further I'll keep this part simpler, I briefly worked in managing the COVID response for the government during COVID and the amount of money that was wasted on unnecessary personnel and supplies horrified me. Managers getting permission to hire more and more "assistants" but giving them various titles to obfuscate what they were really doing, which was offloading all their job duties onto their assistants. It reached a point where I didn't even know what some managers did as they had no job duties left to give away. The government was the true cause of the fuckery. Trump had pitted the states against each other over supplies like it was some form of fucked up Hunger Games. Supplies were fought over not only on a state to state level, but also on a regional state level like Northern and Southern California for instance. States would try to get as many contract RNs as possible, and wouldn't want to give them up, so there were some instances of these contract/travel RNs just getting paid to hang out at various facilities or bases because they were so over staffed.

There was a geriatric couple, I wanna say in their 70s, that lived a few streets down from my parents who called. The call was originally for the husband, who was painfully responsive in the recliner. At that time, we were wearing n95s or MSA1000 masks for every call. (The n95 type we had did not seal on me, so fishbowl it was. Every call.)

The wife immediately had some mocking comments about our appearance and don't we know that COVID is just a hoax and tried to demand us to unmask. Obviously not happening. We were not getting a lot of useful history from her. Oxygen sats in the 60s but respiratory rate and depth was good, so slapped on a non-rebreather with high flow oxygen and prepared to extricate this guy from the basement. Meanwhile, wife still thinks it is more important to tirade about her views on masking and the "fake" illness than worry about her husband who was clearly critically ill whether you believed in it or not. She also wanted us to know that we are "not allowed" to test him for COVID and neither are the hospital.

He's hefty and incontinent of stool, but we hauled him out of the basement on a mega mover. At this point, it should be mentioned that I was the only paramedic on scene. We still had zero health history or medication list or allergies, so I had my EMT partner go back to the wife now that she has had some time to calm down to see if we could get /anything/. She really didn't like me with my MSA1000 mask but tolerated my partner better. Had one or two firefighters go with her because damned if I am sending in my partner alone. Had the remaining ones with me.

So I expect they would be back out shortly, but it is taking a while. Meanwhile, we have switched to bagging the patient because his repsirations were not deep enough and his oxygen saturation had barely gone up. We did not have vents nor protocols for RSI. He might have benefited from BiPAP (carried by our supervisors only), if it weren't already being used on a different critical COVID patient.

I have the side door open for better ventilation and so I could keep an eye on when my partner comes out of the house. When I finally see her, I beckon her to come over so we can get out of here because nothing I'm doing is working and I'm starting to get scared that this guy is gonna code on us. She appeared a little flustered, jogged over to me so I could hear her and she said we had another patient. The wife had passed out, twice. The next unit is 15 minutes away.

My EMT partner gave me the list she had gotten so far and went back inside to join the firefighters to treat the wife. It was a long additional 15 minutes. She did amazing and was able to get a list together for the inbound crew.

I was so thankful when we could finally start moving. I think we were on scene for nearly an hour at that point and our main oxygen tank was getting depleted. I think we had about 150 psi left at the end of that call. No further shenanigans that I remember on the way to the hospital.

Staff told us later when we followed up that the wife continued to deny COVID the entire time and her husband I think went up to the isolation unit once there was room for more

Edit: I forgot to mention he was tubed like immediately once we brought him to the ED.

The EMS I work for is the busiest of our state. We were not hit with the overwhelming surge that some cities/states experienced. I don't have tales of bodies in the hallways. My experience was like that of a sinking ship; I was bailing the water but we just kept slowly sinking.

At the beginning we had a sort of calm before the storm. We had reports it was in our state and people we afraid to call. So we would go longer periods without receiving a call and then suddenly get called to critical patients who really should have called sooner.

We did not have n95s at this stage and were given five general face masks with instructions to wear one for one shift, put it in a paper bag, label the bag with the day, go to the next one with the same set of instructions. By the time of the 5th one it was supposed to be safe to use again. Only, the face masks they gave us were so paper thin that sometimes they didn't last one 12 hr shift, let alone be reused later. Our shitty medical director tried to gaslight us that he can do it just fine so why can't we, and he clearly has a different brand with a thicker material.

Speaking of that director, he made some decisions that led to around 25-30% of the workforce leaving in a year the year before COVID hit, so we were hurting for people bad. The calm didn't last long though.

The administration found that they had a cache somewhere of MSA1000 masks from a post-911 grant or something so that held us over until we could actually get n95s. Those of us who failed the fit test would just continue wearing the MSA1000 mask. I was one of them. Some of my coworkers wouldn't bother and just wore the poor fitting n95s anyway. Like many other places, we only had a couple of n95s per person and you had to make it last. I only got one filter change a year into wearing the MSA1000 for almost every call when I was struggling to breathe just standing with it on.

Then the wave hit. We were constantly on calls now. Some nights we had only 7 ambulances to serve a county of around half a million people. We just didn't have the bodies to handle the volume. I distinctly remember a code being called out a mile away from us and we were already on our way to a respiratory call, and I asked if we should redirect. There was one other ambulance in service that would be 15 minutes away from it. We were told no. Other various moral injuries accumulated from just not having enough resources to get to everyone. I'm sure there were several deaths from this, COVID-related or not.

That summer was the most death I have ever seen. I worked a code about once every three days for around eight weeks that summer. Three of them were kids. Beyond that, just so many DOAs. I saw dozens of dead people. Sure there was a lot of trauma sprinkled in, but a vast majority seemed medical. Strokes were way up. Heart attacks were way up. Weird cardiac stuff post-COVID was abundant.

I have factor v leiden and after seeing how much it seems to just cause hypercoagulopathy, I thought that I could very well be one of the young people at risk of dying of this thing. I had certainly seen many in critical condition at that point. I got about halfway writing an advanced directive to leave for my husband and couldn't finish because I couldn't decide if I want to be put on a vent or not.

By September, people around me in my life were wanting to "go back to normal". It felt so bizarre. I felt like I was fighting with everything I had and then some to help my community through this and.. people just did not give a fuck. They wanted their lives uninterrupted. My experiences was not convenient to their narrative of what was going on.

Even in October, my husband wanted me to go to some Halloween thing with our friends. There was a lull and I did end up going. But I was anxious the entire time. I didn't feel safe. I didn't feel safe for a long time.

I got the vaccine as soon as it was made available to us in December and it soothed my fears just a little. It didn't end there. It kept going. Steady. Bail out the ship and barely stay afloat. The subsequent years were not like the first but it hurts me that people pretended the pandemic is over before we even finished that year

This was maybe the first week of when the first wave hit us. I remember being at one of our big hospitals at dusk (level 1 trauma center, stroke center, burn center, the works). I had to walk nearly a block to my ambulance because there wasn't anywhere else to park because of the sheer volume of ambulances at one hospital. Most were ours, a few from other services.

My captain happened to be parked near mine. He was standing near them while gazing back at the hospital. I joined him and we watched in silence for a minute before another ambulance arrived, lights blazing and breaking the silence. There was no room near the hospital, so they parked by us too. Another COVID patient, by the looks of the full PPE. They made the long treck back to the hospital. The lights were left on and made the distant hospital flicker softly in its hues.

My captain then remarked about how he has never seen such a thing. How this whole scene looks cast straight out of some movie. I agreed, saying it doesn't feel real. We knew this was coming, after seeing the news of various cities hit hard and dirty, and now it was here.

In NYC, we would sometimes pronounce like 10 people a shift. It was outrageous.

We had children with disabilities nursing home just down the road from our ER. Covid got in there and tore the place to pieces. We were getting children all the time. One particular incident I recall we had a baby girl, wasn't even a year old, come into the ER with fever and a nasty cough, but she was all giggles and smiles. The doctor on shift that night was 800% incompetent, and had no fucking clue or care in the world as to what he was doing. Over the course of 3 hours, this beautiful little girl went from smiles and babbles to minimal movement and a locked in 1,000 yard stare. We tried to get IVs. I couldn't, the nurse couldn't, the pediatrician couldn't. I eventually had to put in an IO. The doctor wouldn't do anything for her, and eventually, the head nurse at the time made the call to Medevac her to the nearest pediatric facility about 70 miles away. We had 2 nurses and me (EMT) working that night in a 15-bed ER, with 6 critical patients and 34 non critical. It was a rough night. That next morning, I decided that I've had enough of EMS and turned in my 2 weeks notice a month later. I still work on the ambulance from time to time at my local volunteer fire department, and I get shit on for not taking as many EMS calls as I used to. But that night really crushed my heart. I still don't even know if she's still alive.

I work for FDNY and I was brand new with about 2 months on the street prior to the initial wave of COVID that rocked NYC. It was hell. I will never forget the ominous feeling in the room when the dispatcher said "ladies and gentlemen announcing cad #7000". There is about a month that I don't think the sun came up, I know it did but in my memory it was just gray.

The first interaction with a COVID patient came a day or two earlier. We responded to a call for an 88 y/o male not feeling well, we arrived to what seemed like a normal sick call and assessed the guys vitals. Everything was normal and the guy looked fine so he initially wanted to rma, I was ok with it initially but after talking to him for a few minutes he suddenly looked off. I was able to convince him to go to the hospital just to be safe and upon arrival he was found to have an spo2 of 88% RA (we didn't have pulse oximetry at the time)and his chest x-ray was a mess, he was subsequently intubated and put on a vent. I had to find his family in the waiting room to explain the situation.

The first two weeks of COVID when the call volume was absurdly high was mostly rmas. Tons of people were calling on the suspicion that they may have been exposed. The rma policy was changed such that anyone could rma without olmc approval regardless of the reason for the call and stable patients were encouraged to rma. All of this was prior to us being given pulse oximeters.

The following 3-4 weeks the call volume decreased slightly but all the people we had rma'd the weeks earlier were now on their way to respiratory failure and or cardiac arrest. We would arrive to pts houses (with our new pulse oximeters) to find conscious, alert pts with spo2 readings in the 60's and 70's. Alive pts were transported and promptly intubated by most hospitals. It became commonplace to look at family members and tell them that they should say goodbye before leaving an apartment. The protocol was changed such that pts in cardiac arrest were worked up for 20 minutes and if rosc was not achieved they were pronounced regardless of the level of care of the crew workingit (als, bls, cfr) 20 minutes and done. It was not uncommon to work 2 or 3 arrests in an 8 hour shift. One that stands out was a call for a person with altered mental status, my partner and I found the pt in arrest and performed cpr by ourselves for 20 minutes and pronounced.

I walked into NYP Allen pavilion once to see every single pt in the er intubated and most sharing ventilators. It was erie to only hear the beeps from the ventilators. The director of that er killed herself not long after.

Refrigerated trailers were parked outside every NYC health and hospitals er to store bodies. Most hospitals quickly filled numerous trailers with the bodies stacked in like sardines. One trailer had to be reinforced because the bodily fluids and the weight caused the floor to give out. There was a parking lot on randalls island with 50+ refrigerated trailers waiting. There was talk of opening mass graves to deal with the dead.

We were forced to ration n95 masks out of fear that we would run out (a fear that never came close to fruition) we had to provide a call number and were threatened with discipline if we wore one on a non-approved call type. I lucked out that I had a small stockpile of them in my tech bag that I was able to stretch so I had one for every call.

Most of the department was out at one point or another due to illness. Most of us worked 16 hour days. Entire firehouses were closed due to positive cases amongst members. It got so bad that rather than have engine companies respond to calls the department had two firefighters driving around in pickup trucks to assist us on calls.

The FEMA mutual aid units arrived for the tail end of the shit show and stayed well beyond the end of it. Most of our units went from running nonstop to doing 1 or 2 calls a day. I don't have words for how much we appreciated their help. They were put into the cad system such that they came up first for calls and it gave us all a much needed break. I met some really great people and it really saved a lot of us from the brink.

I don't blame the deniers or the skeptics, as time went on the legitimate emergency ended but the rhetoric didn't. I can only speak for NYC but to me COVID ended in May of 2020. The second and third wave happened but more closely resembled a normal flu season, not the first wave of COVID. The restrictions, the mask mandates, the vaccine mandates and so on far outlived their utility and for many people its a short logical jump from "this is unnecessary now" to "this was never necessary". Things that started out as necessary evils because we didn't know what to do became a symbol for "we're doing something" and they had a severely detrimental and tangible effect on NYC. If you ask anyone who worked here pre and post COVID they will tell you how different things are. People have become unhinged in a way that they just weren't before. Whether you call it a conspiracy or call it an unintended consequence the long term damage is evident. Security theater is a topic that's discussed often in regards to the TSA post 9/11 but it exists post-COVID as well.

I am someone who lived the reality of the COVID-19 pandemic. Reading some of the stories in this thread brought me right back there and i often found myself getting emotional. I saw everything first hand, I know how bad it was but I also saw where things went off the rails. I'm not going to entertain conspiracy theories but I hope this story can bridge the gap a little between those who don't believe it happened and those who don't believe it ended.

We had local hospital throwing out dead bodies in tents because they ran out of room in the freezer trailers. They sat there for a while just casually stacked on top of eachother while security basicallytried to play Tetris with the bodies and make them fit. Ended up making the news.

Our local congressman publicly stated COVID wasn't real, then held a prayer meeting at his church for a firefighter who was hospitalized and intubated because of it. He co-sponsored a bill banning "discrimination of vaccine status" in healthcare, even though I've never seen anyone turned away because they didn't have a vaccine. He made our jobs that much tougher and no amount of "appreciation certificates" will make me forgive him for it.

I volunteered to do some testing outreach clinics in eastern Washington state. This was early on, when vaccines weren't out yet and PPE was scarce. It's August in the desert and I'm standing in a blacktop parking lot without shade wearing plastic ponchos and two sets of gloves (our hands were getting too torn up with such frequent glove changes in the heat, so one set of gloves protected our hands from the sketchy disinfectant and friction from 60 changes a day of the outer gloves). It was hot miserable work. My legs ached, my feet hurt, and after each patient I would have to pour out my elastic PPE sleeves because they were full with 30-50ML of sweat. And at the end of the day, we would tromp back to our hotel to eat a cold meal in our rooms, unable to socialize with each other for safety reasons.

The worst part was that the hotel was owned by a COVID-denyer, so we would have to walk home through these hallways that were just covered in posters with conspiracy theories and stuff on them. I would glare at their desk employees every time I walked in there, tired from trying to save their fucking community while they actively spread the disease we were trying to save them from.

Later, when vaccinations started, I had to go back to that same damn hotel every night under basically the same weather and isolation circumstances, only now I also got to be accused of various anti-vax things too. Spreading AIDS or whatever they came up with. At the end, I WANTED those fuckers to get sick and die. It made me bitter.

Unpaid volunteer labor - every minute of it.

What I always hated was how the public would call us heroes and everything but if you told someone you worked in healthcare they treated you like you were the untouchable. I knew people that wouldn't let their kids play with the kids of my coworkers because they said the house was infected.

2020, first downtime we got after the initial surge, my wife and I had our wedding anniversary. We're both ER Nurses so we were burnt toast. I found a cute bed and breakfast, they had just opened back up post-COVID closures. Anyway. Called, booked reservations, and at the end of the call, thanked them and mentioned we were looking forward to it because the ER had been a zoo the past few weeks. They went silent for a moment and then said they were sorry, but they couldn't take our reservation "out of a concern for the safety" of them and their "other guests" who they didn't want to catch COVID. I mean, I saw a patient three weeks earlier we'd discharged with COVID the next day at Kroger walking around with a mask hanging half off their face. But I guess it shows you how thin that "healthcare heroes" bullshit always was.

I worked in a jail infirmary through the height of COVID. We had 12 healthcare providers on a fully staffed day (ranging from CNAs to APRNs-I was a paramedic.) The average population on any given day was about 1500 inmates. People cycled in and out at all hours of the day and night, and pods were overcrowded. Any attempts we made at trying to isolate or quarantine fell apart because those efforts were "disruptive to the security process" and because the COs, following the trend of most law enforcement here in the south, were primarily Trump Republicans and "didn't believe in COVID."

I made it until November of 2020 before I left following a full-on nervous breakdown.

I just remember how sick people were. I was literally a brand new basic EMT, so I don't think I could appreciate it in the moment but the acuity was wild. The waiting room was packed, always. It was 8 months till I saw a nearly empty waiting room. Suiting up in full get up to run calls in the heat is something I'll never forget. Our service had to ration oxygen at some point. I still have the first N95 I ever got, I was told to keep using it as we had no idea when we could even get more. I used it for 3 months.

It was truly the wild west, kinda the reason I got into EMS. If you ignore the human suffering, I miss it a lot. I miss running back to back to back to back critical pts. I miss the camaraderie. I miss being so thin on resources, asking dispatch for ALS and being told no patient after patient. I miss getting absolutely screamed at by an RN because I was taking the last blanket; her pt needed it, but so did my stretcher for the next call. It wasn't anybody's fault, we was just exhausted. I miss taking ALS transfers on the BLS level because there was literally no one available in our half of the state.

I don't miss how everything in the "real world" sucked ass. I don't miss how the fallout seems to have fucked our country so hard.

I continue to despise those who pretend like it was fake, or 'not that big of a deal'.

I worked as a medic in the south suburbs of Chicago, and our hospitals weren't allowed to go on bypass. There were times I waited for a bed with a very sick patient on my cot for 2-3 hours, all while dispatch was trying to get us to dump the patient because we didn't have any available ambulances due to high call volume. My patients ranged from "I have a cough, take me to the hospital for a COVID test" to "I'm drowning in the own lungs and my oxygen sat is 47%".

My parents and family on my mom's side are all very anti-mask and my parents refused to wear masks at all anywhere. My parents were and still are huge COVID deniers, even though my mom almost died in the hospital from COVID. She was tubed and on a vent for almost a month. I didn't get to see my great grandma before she passed because I knew she was medically fragile, but I was around COVID patients frequently and didn't want to pass anything on to her.

A lot of people died, and many are still dealing with the after effects of having COVID. My mom is on oxygen almost all day and night. She's 47. She knew she was high risk because she had cancer in the past, and her lungs were already in bad condition from her cancer treatments. I had a mental breakdown on Christmas 2021 because my parents wouldn't listen about the masks and vaccines and social distancing because they thought it was stupid and unnecessary, which lead to my mom almost dying, all while I was literally on the front lines dealing with severely sick patients. I risked my own health and safety doing the job that I love because people matter to me, and my parents wouldn't take COVID seriously at all. I refused to visit them because I was so afraid of getting my mom sick and they hated that and told me how stupid I was acting.

I worked night shifts and did my grocery shopping as soon as I'd get off work, and people would literally avoid me like the plague because I was in my uniform that clearly stated I was a paramedic. People would leave the aisles I was in to avoid potentially catching COVID. I felt like I walked around with a bomb strapped to my chest

I started my EMS career a year into COVID. I didn't work 911, but IFT. You always knew when you were going to the Covid floor of a hospital or SNF. It was an entire floor filled to the brim with people diagnosed with Covid. Every hospital had one. You could hear several people on ventilators and others trying to hack up a lung.

My first critical patient was a guy going to a rehab facility post COVID infection, and he ended up having a stroke on the way. Had to turn right back around to the hospital since it was a stroke facility. I had to convince this guy that yes this was serious.

There was always another freaking transport to do as well. Are you sick? Is it COVID? Then come in anyway because we need all the warm bodies we could get. You barely had time to disinfect the truck before being dispatched to another transport.

Everyone was overwhelmed, undersupplied, and exhausted. For me, it was a rude awakening to EMS, but I'm still here and wouldn't give up this job for anything.

Still too soon. I'm still blocking it all out.

Remember the giant walk-in freezer like boxes outside of the ED during early Covid. It was the overflow of Dead bodies since this hospital wasn't huge. Very surreal for a while COVID became a hassle on top of everything else a patient had going on.

Vented stroke pt? They have COVID as well.

Trauma transfer? COVID.

Return to SNF? You guessed it. COVID.

Normal Pt that doesn't have COVID? Nope. They had COVID too.

Wearing shitty trash bag-like gowns, n95 + surgical mask, and double gloves, you'd end up sweating no matter the temperature it was inside or outside.

We ran out of stuff to spray down the patient compartments and had to hand wipe equipment at times with disinfectant wipes. It took ages to clean everything so thoroughly after every patient.

I remember a call where the patient destination was listed as the Convention Center and I had to double check that it was correct because I just didn't understand why they'd be going there...

Turns out the convention center was being used as a field hospital for non-critical COVID patients.

That really stuck with me. I'd been to conventions there multiple times. This is a major metropolitan city in the United States, and you're telling me the convention center I went to growing up is being used as a FIELD HOSPITAL??? It was surreal.

The roads were empty. Not just late at night but nearly all the time. Gone were the multi lane traffic jams that spanned miles.

Everyone was masked..hell I saw people masked and gowned inside their own cars.

The flip side was all the deniers. No masks. No fear. No understanding of how exhausting shuffling COVID patients around was becoming.

How taxing each call became and how much prep and decon went into each transfer.

My partner and I got yelled at on NYE one year by a COVID+ older woman because "we were late picking her up to take her home and now she wouldn't be able to open a bottle of champagne with her daughter at midnight." For context, we were in full ppe, held over, and exhausted from having higher priority transfers as opposed to a simple home discharge.

I also got a complaint filed against me for asking exactly once if the household family members were aware that the PT we brought home to them had COVID, considering no one, including the children and baby that were present, were not isolated or wearing any PPE etc.

We had to reuse n95 masks due to a drastic shortage of supplies.

Each call used so much PPE.

Gown, n95 mask, eye pro, double gloves, surgical mask, and then whoever was driving had to doff all their ppe prior to getting in the cab and put on a whole new set when arriving at the destination.

Also the vent system was ALWAYS running in the back. You couldn't hear shit from anyone let alone your own thoughts or the patient.

One of my old medic partners told me about an SNF that got hit by COVID early on. Most of the residents were in cramped quarters and it ripped through the facility like wildfire. He recalled that most of those people he transferred out of there to area hospitals would end up dying. Very few ever made it back, let alone out of the hospitals.

It's true that COVID may not have been the primary cause of death for many people but it certainly made things much, much worse for those with comorbid conditions.

I remember so many people showing up to ERs for COVID tests of all things..if they didn't have COVID before, they'd likely be leaving with it.

Many people were evaluated and sent home if they didn't have severe respiratory issues or complications from comorbid conditions, but didn't understand why we couldn't accept them all to the hospital/ER.

This went on for years. It felt like time had slowed and everything just stretched out infinitely long. Each shift felt like days. Every week felt like months. A year was a lifetime.

Many people quit. Others killed themselves.

I personally know of a paramedic at an agency I worked for who took their own life while I worked there during the pandemic.

The stress and fears for each other and our families and our patients weighed heavily.

Some strains were laughably tame. Some strains were devastating, leaving people dying on high flow or ventilators or even ECMO with no hope of ever getting weaned off.

The "support" we were shown was a joke to say the least and absolutely insulting and disrespectful at its peak.

"Heroes work here" "Honor our Healthcare Heroes" and similar phrases parroted by so many institutions and people and yet when it came time to support us, to honor us? Silence. Worse than silence. Anger and retaliation towards us for not reaching people faster. For not being there sooner. For not running more calls. For telling people "how to live their lives" when we simply asked for them to mask or socially distance themselves...

EMS week had LESS food/snacks, if anything at all, in the break rooms at hospitals and a 8.5x11 sheet of printer paper "thanking" us.

For all the "thanks", we had even less staffing and support than we had before COVID.

ER wait times, even for sick sick patients could stretch into multiple hours of "holding the wall".

I held the wall once for at least 5hrs. Many other times may not have got the 5hr mark but still fell into the 1-3hr category.

Several times we had to begin interventions while holding the wall as our patients began to decline.

My first priority 4/dead patient, came during COVID. An ICU PT being transferred for hospice after multiple cardiac arrests. We didn't make it out of the parking lot before she rapidly began to Brady down. It was a BLS call and I saw my partner break out the monitor and start applying leads..I hopped in the back to take over while he called the ICU. She became asystolic in front of me. I immediately check her carotid and radial pulse as well as her eyes for pupillary reaction. No pulses, eyes fixed and dilated, asystole on monitor. We took her back up to the ICU where they did another 12L and check for cardiac activity via Ultrasound. Finding no signs of life, they called time of death there in the ICU.

That was the first time I'd had a patient die in my hands.

While she was going for hospice and a DNR, it still is an experience I won't soon forget.

The pandemic was a series of long shifts, little support, and rapidly changing conditions. From week to week and month to month, strains of COVID would change, protocols and best practices for managing these patients would change, and new info and when a vaccine might be available or where to get the next booster shot etc.

Every hospital was overflowing both on the ambo side and waiting room. It wasn't uncommon to have bays filled with more trucks than there were spots for, crews stuck in limbo holding the wall as they waited for not beds, but even just wheelchairs to offload pts into.

There were refrigerator trucks parked in the bays or off to a side for all of the bodies that no longer fit in the hospital morgues.

Everyone was on colors yellow/red/reroute (ER overcrowded/no available cardiac monitored beds/no available beds) which meant no one was because if everyone is crowded then it didn't matter which hospital you went to, the wait times were similar.

The pandemic feels like it was so long ago and like a bad dream but I know it was neither. We were shown very clearly just how razer thin the margins are when it comes to how the modern healthcare system handles major events like a pandemic. It collapsed. Run into the ground. Healthcare team members risked their lives daily without knowing what they were dealing with because if they didn't, they knew more people would die. More than that, they wanted to stop the spread as best as they could to protect their friends and family and loved ones. They were willing to risk not just their health and lives but their sanity. Witnessing the cognitive disconnect between the public's response to the pandemic and the reality they faced each day at work was jarring and painful. The daily battle of non critical patients using up the already limited resources as others fighting for their lives hung on solely on luck whether or not there was enough supplies and staff to try to keep them alive long enough to find some way to cure them before their bodies gave out from trying to fight off the rampant virus that wreaked havoc on their lungs.

Even if they survived COVID and/or time in an ICU or on a ventilator etc, many were found to have permanent deficits as a reminder of their fight with the virus. Scarring of the lungs, reduced lung function, cardiomyopathy from the vaccine, and more effects are still being discovered in relation to COVID. This isn't even including what we now are referring to as "long COVID".

Some of us were lucky and rode out the virus at home with flu like symptoms, loss of smell/taste etc, and others ended up intubated or dead.

You asked for stories of the pandemic. These are just bits and pieces of the experiences of a single EMS clinician in a sea of EMS and Frontline workers who lived and worked through the COVID pandemic. Mine are not isolated experiences. I guarantee you that many others can echo what I saw and went through.

Covid icu doc: We had tons of venous and arterial clots. One patient we had had Covid ARDS on 100% APRV vent settings and bilateral pneumothoraces. Also misfortunate enough to have two bilateral ischemic limbs from arterial clots. Needed amputation but too sick. We stuck them in dry ice baths like old school battlefield medicine to try to encourage dry gangrene so we could do bedside amputation soon. The pain must have been excruciating and we had him maxed on ketamine and fentanyl infusion. He never made it that far. On top of that it was an open make shift Covid ward where the only thing separating patients were make shift sheet walls. Codes if people dying happened every day during the delta wave if 2021. It must have been terrifying watching through the cracks of those sheets seeing your neighbor die.